1960s Childhood

Moon Landings, The Kinks and the 1966 World Cup

1960s Childhood

Moon Landings, The Kinks and the 1966 World Cup

DEREK TAIT

AMBERLEY

First published 2014

Amberley Publishing
The Hill, Stroud
Gloucestershire, GL5 4EP

www.amberley-books.com

British Library Cataloguing in Publication Data.
A catalogue record for this book is available from the British Library.

ISBN 978 1 4456 3762 4 (paperbook)
ISBN 987 1 4456 3775 4 (ebook)

Typeset in 10pt on 12.5pt Sabon.
Typesetting and Origination by Amberley Publishing.
Printed in the UK.

Contents

Introduction

The 1960s is one of the most fondly remembered decades. It brought a time of change, leaving behind the rationing of the war years, and a great improvement to many people's lives. For the first time, many people had their own cars, central heating, hot water, wall-to-wall carpets and inside toilets.

At the beginning of the 1960s, most families lived in rented accommodation, and very few owned their own houses. There was no central heating, houses were draughty and most homes didn't have telephones. Many didn't have a television and the ones that did rented them.

Later, modern appliances in the home included washing machines, fridge-freezers, vacuum cleaners and cookers. All made the lives of mothers and housewives a lot easier.

There was an explosion of pop music started by bands such as The Beatles, The Rolling Stones, The Kinks and The Who. The Beatles opened the door for the 'British Invasion', which took the US record charts by storm. The Beatles were followed by screaming fans wherever they went, especially when they first landed on American soil in 1964, where there had been a huge demand for their single 'I Want to Hold Your Hand', which had sold an incredible 1.5 million copies in America in just three weeks.

New fashions brought colour to people's lives, with miniskirts and maxi skirts, hot pants, corduroys, snazzy shirts and cravats, winkle-picker shoes and the influence of clothes worn by rockers, mods and hippies including tie-dye and batik fabrics, bell-bottoms and paisley prints.

Television fitted in well with the new colourful pop era, although most households only had black-and-white sets and there were only three channels to watch. Classic shows included *The Avengers*, *The Man from U.N.C.L.E.* and *Lost in Space*, and for children there were *Crackerjack*, *Blue Peter* and many more. Gerry Anderson brought children a wealth of exciting new shows, such as *Stingray*. TV would never be the same again. Even the adverts were classics; this was the era of the PG chimps, who were imitated by children in schoolyards throughout the land.

Shows featuring the latest pop music included *Ready, Steady, Go!* hosted by Keith Fordyce, and music papers such as *The New Musical Express* carried all the news of the latest bands, together with pictures of pop stars to pin on your bedroom wall.

Some of the best-remembered toys were made for children in the 1960s. These included all-time classics such as Action Man, yo-yos, and Lego. Plastic Airfix, Frog or Revell kits of aeroplanes, ships and spacecraft were also incredibly popular with boys. Board games were hugely popular; some of the best included Mouse Trap and Scrabble.

A trip to the cinema was a real treat. When popular films were shown, queues would form around the block and, once inside, the cinema would be packed.

School life involved strict discipline and would start at 9 a.m. with morning prayers and assembly. Classes were orderly, with the threat of the cane for anyone who misbehaved. Lessons would involve maths, English, geography, history, French and PE at junior school, with a whole range of other subjects at secondary school, depending on gender. Most children walked to school and it was uncommon for someone's parents to drop them off in the car.

Holidays abroad were unheard of. Camping and caravan trips were popular, as were visits to holiday camps such as Butlin's and Pontin's. A holiday at Butlin's was designed to give the whole family a rest, with meals and entertainment laid on and someone to look after the children in the evenings. The thrill of free fairground rides such as the dodgems had children everywhere pestering their parents to take them.

World events, such as the assassination of John F. Kennedy in 1963, affected everyone. The thrill of the World Cup in 1966, as Geoff Hurst scored a hat-trick leading to England beating West Germany 4-2, will never be forgotten. The win is still remembered fondly, as are the players who took part.

The moon landings at the end of the 1960s had everyone gathered around their television sets waiting with anticipation as Neil Armstrong set foot on the moon with the immortal words, 'That's one small step for man, one giant leap for mankind.' Televisions all over the land remained on, as live footage of the astronauts on the moon was beamed back to Earth. Everyone was fascinated with the moon landings, and there were endless memorabilia and souvenirs available, including plastic space models, records featuring the voices of the astronauts, and replica astronaut helmets for boys. Television reflected the new space craze.

Growing up in the 1960s offered much excitement for children. What with the fun of exploring the area, playing outdoors, riding bikes, building dens and go-karts, climbing trees and playing football in the street, there was never a dull moment and it was only brought to an end when your mum called you in for tea.

The 1960s was a special time and one that will never be repeated for innovation, fashion, television and music. For a child, it was the best of times.

1

Home Life

At the beginning of the 1960s, Harold Macmillan was the Prime Minister of Great Britain and Elizabeth II had been queen since 1952. At home, most families lived in rented accommodation; very few owned their own houses. There was no central heating, houses were draughty and most didn't have telephones.

In comparison to today, homes in the early 1960s were quite basic. There was no double glazing, there were no duvets, and the only heating came from the modern gas or electric fire in the front room.

Although it was now the 1960s, at the beginning of the decade there were still houses with outside toilets and no bathrooms. Most homes were heated by a coal fire in the front room, and the coal man would deliver regularly. On cold winter days, the smell of chimney smoke filled the air. Windows were single-glazed, with wooden frames, which meant that rooms were colder and draughtier in the winter months. Frost would form on the inside of windows on the chilliest days.

Many families lived in terraced houses and were friendly with their neighbours. However, the 1960s saw the building of numerous blocks of flats, which were seen as an answer to housing problems but led to a loss of the community spirit that had been rife in the 1950s, and also meant that children had no gardens and nowhere to play.

Most fathers had jobs that started at 9 a.m. in the morning

and most mothers stayed at home to look after the children, if they were of preschool age, and to do the housework, which included washing clothes without a washing machine, cleaning without a vacuum cleaner and all the other chores for which we have appliances nowadays.

If the children were of school age, they would be fed, got ready and dressed and walked to school to be there for 9 a.m. The father in the household would set off earlier to catch the train or bus, or would cycle or walk to work. At the beginning of the 1960s, there were still few cars. However, life changed greatly over the decade.

Policemen patrolled the area on foot and were respected. There was no backchat from children, and many minor misdemeanours, such as pinching apples or being cheeky, could find a kid in trouble with the local 'bobby' and marched home to their parents for a telling off. Policemen would also see that children were crossing the road correctly and some would be awarded certificates at school if they were seen to 'look right, look left and look right again' before crossing. Adverts featuring Tufty the Squirrel were shown on television to raise awareness. Children were told off by the local bobby if they were seen running across the road without looking.

Adults were referred to by their titles, Mr or Mrs, and teachers were referred to as 'Sir' or 'Miss'. Children were taught to be polite, saying 'please' and 'thank you', and picked up if they said 'yeah' instead of 'yes'.

Mothers, grans and aunties all knitted, and there would be plenty of warm hats, gloves, balaclavas and jumpers for the whole family. At the time, it was a lot cheaper to knit than to buy knitted goods from the shop. The click-clack of knitting needles could be heard everywhere, even when watching television, waiting for a film to start at the cinema or sitting on the bus. The make and mend ideal of the war still carried on and most things were fixed, if they could be, rather than thrown away. Socks would be re-darned and holes in jumpers, etc., would be repaired.

When not at school, children could be seen playing out in the street, kicking a ball around, riding home-made go-karts, on roller skates or bikes, or playing hopscotch or other similar games. If there was a spare wall, girls would be standing on their hands upside down against it or doing cartwheels. Others skipped or played tag. Most backstreets still weren't bothered much by traffic, so having a game of football was seen as quite safe. Parks, fields and woods were all considered safe places to play, and parents had no worries about their children being out and about enjoying themselves as long as they didn't get up to any mischief.

As in the 1950s, many households left their doors unlocked when they were in, and neighbours would pop around for a cup of tea or a chat. More people were seen in the street either talking with their neighbours or travelling to the local corner shop for essentials. The shopkeeper would know everyone in the area and would be friendly with most. Many shopkeepers offered 'tick', which meant that people could pay later when they had the money.

Every morning, the milkman and the postman would both call early, long before it was time to set off to work or school, and it was common for everyone to have their milk delivered; it arrived in glass bottles which were left on the doorstep. Most milk was delivered by a milkman driving a slow-moving electric-powered open van. However, some deliveries in the early 1960s were still made using horses and carts.

Other visitors to the home would include the rent man. Most people rented their homes and paid weekly. Salesmen would call to sell their wares, which could include anything from brushes to the *Children's Encyclopaedia Britannica*. The encyclopaedia was sold as a must for children's education, and many families paid regularly to build up the complete collection of books. Other salesmen would call trying to sell housewives the latest time-saving appliances, such as modern labour-saving vacuum cleaners. Callers would also include the gas and electric man, who would visit to read the meters. Many people had coin-operated electric meters, which originally took pennies.

The most popular visitor to the street, for children, was the ice cream man. All children would rush outside when the chimes of his van were heard, to get either an ice cream or the latest lolly, which featured names such as Fab, Rocket and Zoom. Several of them came with free picture cards or badges. The cards could be collected in booklets or on wallcharts that could be pinned to bedroom walls.

The interiors of homes were modestly decorated at the beginning of the 1960s, but this all changed as the decade moved on. Rooms became more colourful, with more modern furniture in keeping with the time. Wacky wallpaper, featuring a huge variety of colours and patterns, appeared in homes all over the country. Whereas the fireplace had been the previous focus of the front room, the seating was now placed to focus on the television set. Sofas, sometimes in bright colours, would include scatter cushions with bright colourful patterns or flowers. David Hicks, an English designer, had a direct influence on the interiors of homes, with fabrics inspired by India. Later in the 1960s, especially at the time of flower power and the hippy movement, psychedelic patterns and acid-edged colours appeared. The space programme also had an effect on interiors, with the introduction of white pod-shaped seats as well as round white plastic space-age televisions. These weren't appealing to everyone, though. Television programmes of the day provide an insight into the interiors of some homes in the later 1960s; the best examples are probably *The Avengers*, *The Prisoner*, and *The Saint*. Colours that were wild and vibrant were acceptable then, but wouldn't appeal to many nowadays. Teak and wood-effect furniture, such as Formica, became popular, as did large table lamps, colourful pottery and modern-shaped chairs, including swivel chairs, in modern fabrics.

Kitchens featured colourful Formica tops and vinyl flooring tiles in a chessboard-type pattern, together with new, modern units to store food. Kitchens were arranged so that the latest appliances such as cookers, fridges and washing machines could all fit in well. Some kitchens had portable radios so that Mum could listen to her favourite station while cooking the meals or doing other household chores. Storage jars, plates, bowls and other kitchen pottery ware now came with colourful designs featuring wild vibrant patterns as well as vivid flowers of orange, yellow, red and blue. Wall tiles came in various colours but most people seemed to have white ones. Electric kettles were uncommon, and most people boiled their water on the stove.

The kitchen would also be the place where clothes would be washed and ironed. However, the old scrubbing boards and mangles of the 1950s had long gone, even though some households probably still used them. Larger kitchens featured Formica tops to eat at together with bar-stool-type seats made of chrome and leather.

The more adventurous house even had its own bar, complete with drinks, ideal for entertaining guests. Wood panelling on walls also became popular, although, again, it didn't appeal to everyone.

Bedrooms were warmer, with fitted carpets and colourful curtains, and featured modern fabrics and up-to-date furniture. If the bedroom belonged to a teenager, the room might also include a Dansette record player, a transistor radio and pictures of the latest pop or film stars on the wall. Central heating meant that many rooms now had their own adjustable radiators and more time was spent in other rooms in the house rather than everyone just gathering in the main living room. Bedroom furniture included laminated wood, or pine, wardrobes, chest of drawers and bedside tables. Wooden bunk beds were popular with children who had to share a room. The dark furniture which had been popular in the 1950s, and before, was now replaced with much lighter, modern furniture.

Habitat opened in 1964. Founded by Terence Conran, the first store opened in Fulham Road in Chelsea and sold Conran's Summa range of furniture. Although not readily available to everyone, the products had a knock-on effect on the type and style of furniture that was available in the 1960s. Lava lamps took off in the decade, as did bean bags and shagpile rugs. Paintings on the wall included 6s 6d pictures from Woolworths, some of which featured seascapes from Cornwall complete with seagulls. Colourful ceramics adorned the fireplace which probably contained an electric or modern gas fire. Plastic brick-effect surrounds were all the rage for a while.

Bathrooms now featured fitted baths (no more sitting in front of the fire in a tin bath), a washbasin and an inside toilet, which came in blues, pinks, greens and other colours. Most bathrooms were carpeted and wallpapered, and if they didn't have their own radiator, a three-bar electric fire was used (although highly unsafe). Bath time was now a luxury rather than a chore. Showers were still a long way in the future for most families in the UK.

By the end of the 1960s, nearly every family had its own television, washing machine, a fridge with a freezer compartment, and many of the other appliances that we take for granted nowadays. Home telephones became more popular, although many people didn't have them until the 1970s. Most people now had an indoor bathroom, and many had central heating and wall-to-wall carpet. More women went to work each day and the routine of the daily chores in the household changed completely. One of the biggest changes was that people now had their own cars, which made it easier to travel back and forwards to work and also meant more trips to the country and seaside. However, most children still walked to school or caught the bus.

When everyone returned home later in the day, they would have their evening meal at the table, either in the front room or kitchen. Sitting watching the television with your tea on your lap was unheard of. Everyone sat around the table while Dad probably told his family the sort of day he had, as did Mum, and the kids told of their day at school and anything that had happened. In the new television age, children were quite fidgety, eager to finish their meal so that they could leave the table and sit in front of the box to watch their favourite programmes.

By the end of the 1960s, the home was a cosy place, with modern appliances, warm rooms, colourful decoration, plenty to eat and inside bathrooms. Most families could only watch television in black and white, but then you can't have everything!

2

Food

Television, cinema and magazine advertising all influenced the sweets and chocolates bought in the 1960s. Brightly coloured wrappers and free gifts such as badges were all made to appeal to children. Many areas had their own sweet shop or newsagents selling sweets and chocolate. They were often displayed in huge jars, which were measured out on scales before being put in a small paper bag for the customer. Boiled sweets, bonbons, chocolate mice, liquorice, black jacks and fruit salads were all favourites, and eight of the latter could be bought for 1*d*.

Collecting was always very popular with children. Cards came in packs with a strip of bubblegum. Many featured popular television shows of the day, including *Danger Man*, *The Man from U.N.C.L.E.* and *Star Trek*, or music stars and footballers. Movies also had their own bubblegum cards; the *Goldfinger* cards came with free 007 badges. By collecting the wrappers of some of the cards, such as those of *Captain Scarlet*, free posters of favourite television characters, which were ideal for bedroom walls, could be sent for. You never knew which cards you were getting when you bought them, so many children would end up with lots of doubles which they would happily swap in the playground. Unscrupulous manufacturers deliberately printed more of some cards and less of others so that collecting the whole set was more difficult and more costly.

Bazooka Joe bubblegum was also popular, and came with

a free cartoon comic strip. Again, by collecting the strips, you could send away for a range of products such as binoculars and cameras. They were all cheaply made and from Hong Kong, but children still found it very exciting. The gifts soon fell apart!

Favourite chocolates of the time included All Chocolate Treets, which were first marketed in the 1960s. They came in yellow packets and the television advert for the product, first shown in 1967, featured the memorable slogan 'Melts in your mouth, not in your hand'. Milky Bars were loved by children, and the television advert featured a blonde boy, complete with round glasses and dressed as a cowboy, announcing, 'The Milky bars are on me!' Topic's well-remembered advert featured the slogan 'A hazelnut in every bite'.

Animal Bars featured a different animal on the label, and these could be cut out and stuck in a special album from Nestlé. It appealed to the collector that was inside every child.

In 1969, Mars carried the slogan 'Maxis from Mars', and there was a chance to win one of number of white Maxi cars being given away by the company. All you had to do was match the number printed inside the wrapper of a Mars bar to the number featured on a particular car, which could be seen driving around various towns and cities.

Other chocolate brands associated with television adverts included Cadbury's Flake, featuring the Flake girl; Bounty, again featuring a bikini-clad girl but this time on a desert island; and Turkish Delight, featuring a girl in Arab costume with the slogan 'Full of Eastern Promise'.

Many chocolates and sweets from the 1960s are still around today, including Smarties, Toffee Crisp, and Maltesers. Marathon later became Snickers, but remained much the same. Caramac has now also made a comeback.

Skippy was launched in 1960. It featured caramel with a wafer centre, and its advertising slogan was 'It's got a crunch in the biscuit and a munch in the middle'. A television advert showed a couple in swinging London pulling up on a scooter outside a trendy coffee bar and going inside for their Skippys.

Aztec was launched in 1967, and was made of milk

chocolate, nougat and caramel. It was very popular at the time.

Cadbury's Toffee Buttons were aimed at children and were also launched in 1967. They featured brightly coloured cowboys and Indians on the wrapper, which appealed to kids of the day because of the many westerns that were shown on television at the time.

The Dairy Crunch advert featured Spike Milligan appealing for people to vote for him for prime minister instead of Harold Wilson. In the comical advert, he promised a free Dairy Crunch bar for every vote.

Mums got boxes of chocolates on special occasions and these included Milk Tray, whose television advert featured a handsome man making an impossible journey over land and sea to deliver a box of chocolates to the one he loved, leaving only his calling card. It was all very James Bond.

Christmas brought a selection of chocolates in special stockings or 'selection boxes', complete with a cardboard insert that often could be cut out and made into a puppet.

Sweet cigarettes were loved by children. They all came in imitation cigarette boxes, and kids, especially boys, would emulate their favourite film and television stars (or dad and older brother) by pretending to smoke. Of course today they're not allowed to be called sweet cigarettes, and are known as 'candy sticks'. Each sweet cigarette had a red tip on the end to make it appear as if it was lit. The packets promoted television shows, movies and cartoons, and the most popular featured *Dixon of Dock Green*, *Chitty Chitty Bang Bang*, and *Joe 90*. Each pack came with cards, which were collected and swapped to get the full set. Albums could also be bought, in which you would stick the cards.

Chocolate and sweets were sold individually in the 1960s, and were seen as a treat. There were no multipacks like there are today. For a kid, a trip to the sweet shop or to a newsagent to buy chocolate was somehow more special, and manufacturers made sure they promoted their product with bright packaging, advertising and numerous free gifts.

Most shopping was bought from the corner shop, which

supplied nearly everything a household needed. The majority of items were kept behind the counter; the shopper asked for what they wanted and the assistant went and fetched it. Most items weren't wrapped or pre-packaged, and had to be measured out and wrapped in the shop. It was common for people to ask for half a loaf of bread, or to have items such as cheese cut and weighed in front of them. Many people met up there, chatted about anything that was going on in their lives and, in general, the atmosphere was very friendly. However, the whole process was very labour intensive (for the assistant) and could be slow going. This was the way it had been for many years but by the 1960s, supermarkets had started to become more popular. Self-service supermarkets were already common in other countries such as America, but in Britain, it took much longer for them to become established. In 1947, only ten self-service shops existed in the UK. In the 1950s, the first supermarket, under the new Premier Supermarkets brand, opened in Streatham. It was soon taking ten times more profit than the usual general shops, and other store owners wanted to take advantage of the situation. Jack Cohen opened his first Tesco general shop in 1932 and went on to open one of the first supermarkets, which led, eventually, to it becoming the huge empire it is today.

Sugar and meat consumption was at an all-time high during the 1960s. This was partly due to the rationing of food during the Second World War, which had carried on well into the 1950s. Tinned foods proved very convenient, making meals easy to prepare. Heinz Baked Beans were a kids' favourite, and the television advert stating 'Beanz Meanz Heinz' is fondly remembered by many.

Many towns and cities in the UK had no large supermarkets in the 1960s, although larger grocer's shops such as Liptons, Mace, the Co-op and Supreme were common. Woolworths also sold some food, as well as many other products.

Many shops, as well as garages, offered Green Shield stamps, which were collected and stuck in a book. When you had filled several books, you could redeem a gift from their catalogue and collect it from a local store. In a similar way, the Co-op gave their customers blue stamps, which could be redeemed for money when a book was full.

As a child, the first piece of food packaging seen in the morning was the cereal packet. Throughout the 1960s, clever designs and free gifts were used to attract children to the product. Over the decade, boxes featured characters from films and television shows. Cartoon characters on cereal packets were also a favourite. Kellogg's Cornflakes included pirates, cowboys and Indians, and cut-out masks on the rear of the packets. Shredded Wheat included scenes on the back of the packet from the popular television series *Tarzan*, with rub-down Letraset transfers inside the packet.

Sugar Smacks were very sweet, and popular with children. Free gifts included badges from *Star Trek* and *Captain Scarlet* and toys from *Thunderbirds*. Sugar Puffs gave away a range of toys including Wild West models, model cars and slides featuring the space programme. They all ran many competitions, including one to win a full-size Dalek. On Kellogg's Frosties, there were mail-away offers which involved collecting six cardboard lids to send away for a model of a car or aircraft or something similar. There were many other cereals which all vied for the attention of children including Rice Krispies, Ricicles (featuring Noddy), and Cubs (mini Shredded Wheat).

While eating breakfast, toast would be spread with butter and Robertson's jam. By collecting the coupons on the label, a child could send away for either a golliwog statuette or a golliwog badge. This appealed greatly to children. To get a statuette, the tokens would have to be sent off with 1s to cover postage. There was much excitement when it arrived in a small box packed with straw. Each golliwog was hand painted, and there were various band members as well as footballers.

As well as Robertson's, there was Hartley's jam, and Gale's honey. Robertson's also made Silver Shred marmalade. A favourite with children was Lyle's Golden Syrup.

Brooke Bond tea cards were very popular with children. Every time mum bought a box of tea, there would be much excitement to see which tea card was inside. These were then stuck in an album. In the 1960s, there were various sets to collect. Many in the early 1960s were nature based, and included Freshwater Fish, Tropical Birds, African Wildlife, Asian Wildlife, British Butterflies, Wildflowers in Britain, Wild Birds in Britain and Trees in Britain. From 1967, the titles moved away from nature and included British Costume, Flags & Emblems of the World, History of the Motor Car, and Famous People. The PG Tips brand of tea also appealed to children because of the company's many adverts on television featuring chimpanzees together with their comic antics. The adverts featured the voices of actors of the day and made the chimps appear to be talking. Voice-overs were provided by Peter Sellers, Bob Monkhouse and Bernard Cribbins. The advert featuring chimps as removal men, with the classic lines 'Cooee, cooee Mr Shifter. Light refreshment', and 'Dad, do you know the piano's on my foot? – You hum it, son, and I'll play it', has become a classic. Promotional items were given away with the tea including badges and handkerchiefs. Most tea came loose, in a box; there were teabags but hardly anyone used them.

Packaged sliced bread became more popular in the 1960s. In 1961, a new process introduced a way of aerating bread that made it quicker and easier to produce a loaf. Many small bakers were bought up by larger firms. Popular manufacturers of bread were Mother's Pride, Hovis, Nimble and Slimcea.

Nimble was advertised for slimmers, and the television advert showed a girl being lifted in the air by a hot-air balloon. The television advert featured the well-remembered lyrics 'She flies like a bird in the sky', which were from the song 'I Can't Let Maggie Go', a hit for Honeybus in 1968. The girl featured in the Nimble advert was Emily Jones.

Mother's Pride's slogan was 'Mother's Pride's a family, a family of bread'. One popular television advert for the brand featured Dusty Springfield.

Margarines were now largely used, and were seen as healthier and a way to slim. One of the best known was Stork, whose advertising campaign asked, 'Can you tell the difference between Stork and butter?' Their television advert would show someone testing people in the street to see if they could tell the difference. There was a parody printed which featured a photo of The Monkees' Peter Tork next to a chimpanzee. The caption asked, 'Can you tell Tork from Mutter?'

Other products made to appeal to children included Angel Delight (which came in strawberry, chocolate and banana flavours), Instant Whip and Dream Topping. Blancmange was also well liked and came in small boxes. Other afters-type dishes included Chiver's Jelly (ideal for children's parties), Birds Eye Raspberry, Strawberry or Lemon Mousse, and Ambrosia Rice Pudding.

Yoghurt was introduced in the 1960s, but came in one flavour, plain, and didn't appeal to many people. One of the first manufacturers was Ski. In a period when many similar foods contained a lot of sugar, yoghurt was seen to taste a bit sour. The product caught on later when different flavours were introduced.

Popular snacks included Smiths potato crisps in various flavours, twiglets, and KP salted peanuts.

With most fridges only having a small freezer compartment, fish fingers became one of the first popular frozen items and appealed to children. Blocks of ice cream could be bought from the ice cream van and also stored there, but that was often its full capacity.

Later, as freezers grew, Birds Eye, Findus and Ross all geared up to provide a new range of frozen food for the whole family.

Cadbury's launched Smash, a type of instant potato, in the 1960s. All that was needed was to add hot water, which saved Mum a great deal of time mashing proper potatoes. The brand really took off in the early 1970s.

Certain parts of the country saw a dramatic rise in Indian restaurants at this time, and the taste for purely British food in the UK changed. Vesta Beef Curry was one of the first complete meals in a box, and was a treat at mealtimes. Vesta Chow Mein soon followed.

Sauces included Heinz Tomato Sauce, HP and Daddies Brown Sauce. Oxo, Bovril and Bisto were all used to make gravy, and had been for many years.

For children, there were themed chocolate biscuits, such as the *Joe 90* chocolate wafer. Special boxes of biscuits were produced for Christmas.

To drink, children loved Nesquik, which came in various flavours. Other popular drinks were Cadbury's Bournville Cocoa, Horlicks and Ovaltine. The Corona man would also deliver pop in glass bottles. Many kids made sure they saved the 'empties', as they could redeem 2*d* on them when they gave them back. Some even went looking for discarded ones so that they could boost their pocket money. Corona came in many flavours including lemonade, orangeade, strawberry and later dandelion and burdock and cream soda. The drink was promoted on television in the 1960s by singer and comedian, Dave King. Other fizzy drinks available at the time included Coca Cola, Fanta, and Lucozade. Lucozade came in one flavour, which many kids didn't like, but it was seen as a drink to pick you up when you were ill because it contained so much glucose.

Household cleaning products included Brillo soap pads, Ajax and Domestos. For washing machines, there was Fairy Snow, Radiant, and Omo washing powder.

With air travel becoming more common, fruits and vegetables from abroad were appearing in shops. Many would have been impossible to grow in the UK at certain times of the year because of the climate and had previously only been available seasonally.

Tupperware was seen as the place to store unwanted food, and was ideal for picnics. Many housewives organised Tupperware parties in the 1960s and there seemed to be a different-shaped container for everything.

Television chefs appeared more and more on the box as the choice of food grew. At the beginning of the decade, Fanny and Johnny Craddock had been well watched, and towards the end of the 1960s, Graham Kerr, the Galloping Gourmet, hosted one of the most watched television cookery programmes.

As the 1960s moved on, products were geared towards newer appliances. More people had washing machines, the latest gas and electric cookers and fridge-freezers.

Household shopping and the types of food bought changed greatly during the 1960s, and led to a whole new range of food, which is reflected in what we eat today. With it came a new age of packaging and promotion, and many brands became household names.

3

Technology

The greatest technological achievement of the 1960s was landing men on the Moon during July 1969. When Neil Armstrong first set foot on the Moon, it came at the end of a space programme that had seen unmanned craft, dogs and monkeys sent into space, orbits of the earth and several moon-walks and spacewalks. Many of the achievements had been made by the USSR, which led to a race with America to put the first man on the Moon.

Yuri Gagarin took the first human space flight in 1961 on board the Vostok 1. The Soviets followed this with the first spacewalk, by Aleksei Leonov, in 1965. Previously, the first unmanned craft in space was the USSR's Sputnik 1 in 1957. There was much anticipation and thrill throughout the 1960s with the progression of the space programme and there was much excitement as live images of the Apollo astronauts on the Moon were broadcast on television towards the end of the decade.

The patent for the laser was granted in 1960. Today, lasers have many uses, including in consumer devices such as optical disc drives, barcode scanners and laser printers. They are also used in surgery and for cutting and welding materials. The word laser stands for Light Amplification by Stimulated Emission of Radiation.

Other advances during the 1960s included the invention of the audio compact cassette in 1962. Cassette players came out much later in the UK, and, for a while, everyone had one. They were portable and had a handle so they could easily be carried around. Many children were bought them by their parents for passing their eleven-plus exam or for birthdays or Christmas. There was much fun to be had taping Pick of the Pops on Radio 1 or Top of the Pops from the television, although everyone had to stay quiet because the machine picked up every sound. For a long while, the cassette competed with the vinyl LP but, as with the LP, disappeared for good with the birth of the digital age.

The first touch-tone telephones were introduced in 1963, although many households in the UK didn't even have a regular phone and when they did get one, more towards the end of the 1960s or later, they all came with dials. Touch-tone, at the time, was more an American thing.

The first computer mouse was invented in 1964 by Douglas Engelbart. Originally, it was made from wood, complete with two gear wheels. It would be over thirty years before they were commonly used. There were no home computers in the 1960s; those used by large companies were basic, compared to today, and took up a lot of space.

The first intercity train was used in 1966, making travel much quicker and cleaner. The new train used electricity rather than coal or diesel as had previously been the case.

The first video game console was invented in 1966 by Ralph Baer, who played the first two-man game in 1968 (he lost!). It was a while before video games were made commercially, with Computer Space being the first coin-operated video machine in 1971. Home video games didn't take off until 1975 when Atari's Pong (a tennis-type game) was introduced.

Donald Campbell broke the world speed limit, achieving 320 mph, on Lake Coniston on 4 July 1967, but was killed instantly. The vehicle he was travelling in, the *Bluebird K7*, flipped over and broke up. It was many years before the vehicle and the body of Donald Campbell were found.

BBC Two began transmitting the first colour television pictures in the UK in 1967. However, many people were still watching in black and white, and it was quite a few years before colour sets were widely used. Colour televisions were incredibly expensive when they first appeared on the market. Even though most people watched the transmission of the first colour pictures on their black-and-white televisions, it was apparent that many of the presenters, including men, had been heavily made up for the occasion, with bright lipstick and other make-up.

Dynamic Access Random Memory first appeared in 1968. The Toshiba BC-1411 electronic calculator, which first appeared in November 1966, used a form of dynamic RAM in its components. Dynamic Access Random Memory would later play a major part in the components of the modern computer.

The first pelican crossings were introduced in 1969. They featured push buttons to change the lights. A green man would illuminate if it was safe to cross the road and a red man would illuminate if it wasn't. There were various adverts on television at the time, showing people how to use them properly. The best-remembered advert featured a cartoon with the voice of Deryck Guyler. It showed a man teaching his granddaughter how to use the new crossing. They manage to cross safely, but the man leaves his umbrella behind and the advert ends with the memorable phrase 'Oh, it's started to rain. Wish I'd brought me brolly!'

The teasmade was a very popular item for a while. The thought of waking up in the morning and having a cup of tea made for you, without getting out of bed, seemed very appealing. It was all very space age. The Green Shield Stamp shop would even give you a free one if you saved enough stamps. Eventually, it became clear that a cup of tea from a machine could never be like the real thing, and teasmades seemed to suddenly disappear from all homes.

The clock/radio seemed the ideal gadget to keep beside your bed. Not only would you know the time but you could also listen to all your favourite sounds on the radio. Some had alarms to wake you up in the morning. In later years, they included digital clocks and cassette units and eventually, much later, took CDs.

The first supersonic test flight, in the Anglo-French airliner Concorde, took place in 1969. The Concorde entered service in 1976 and was grounded in 2003 after a serious crash in 2000 which killed all passengers on board. Air France and British Airways cited the reason for the withdrawal as low passenger numbers due to the earlier crash and the 9/11 attacks.

Of course, everyday objects like cars, televisions, fridges, washing machines, cookers, etc., all changed greatly over the decade and, by the end of the 1960s, many of these luxuries were seen to be very modern. Many of the everyday products that we use today evolved from objects that were novelties back in the 1960s.

At the beginning of the 1960s hardly anyone had a car, but by the end of the decade most families owned one.

The decade is mostly summed up by one particular automobile, the Mini, which became an icon of the 1960s. The car was designed by Sir Alec Issigonis and was manufactured at the Longbridge and Cowley plants in England as well as later being produced in other countries all around the world. The first model appeared in 1959 and sold in its thousands. It was seen as a small, low-cost, about-town car which was also suitable for families. It was marketed by Austin and Morris until 1969.

Sportier versions included the Mini Cooper and Mini 'S' which went on to win the Monte Carlo Rally four times between 1964 and 1967. They famously appeared in the Michael Caine film *The Italian Job* in 1969, and they were popularised throughout the decade by pop stars, film and television stars and models (including Twiggy). The police also used various models of Minis as their patrol cars.

The 1960s had some other very memorable cars, however, including the Ford Cortina. The Cortina was first made in 1962 and by the 1970s, was Britain's bestselling car.

If you were well-off, the car to have was an E-Type Jaguar, which came out in 1961 and cost an incredible £2,197. To put that in context, the average cost of a house in 1961 was £2,770. Sports cars stood out in the 1960s, as most people, if they owned a car at all, had a car suited to their family. There were some very sporty models available in the 1960s and many are fondly remembered but they were seen mainly on the television being driven by people like the Saint. Sought-after sports cars included the Triumph TR4, the Austin Healey Frogeye Sprite, and, of course, Simon Templar's car, the Volvo P1800.

The Volkswagen Beetle was also popular in the 1960s and, unusually, came with an engine in the back. Like the Mini, it was a great about-town car. As with VW campers, they were later associated with the hippy movement, although most people who had them in Britain used them as family cars.

Other classic cars of the 1960s included the Fiat 124 (the European Car of the Year in 1967), the Alfa Romeo Duetto (first produced in 1966 and famously featured in *The Graduate*), and the Ford Zephyr.

Many older cars remained on the road and it wasn't unusual to see vehicles from the 1920s, 1930s, 1940s or 1950s still driving about.

Petrol companies did all they could to attract customers, with many free gifts that appealed to children. Esso's 'Put a Tiger in your Tank' campaign offered free badges and imitation tiger tails for kids. Many tiger tails could be seen on bikes or fixed to the wing mirror of cars at the time. Esso also offered other gifts featuring the Esso tiger, including beakers, cups, trays and a range of other items. Shell offered similar gifts, including glass tumblers, which could be redeemed by collecting tokens (one was given for every 5 gallons of petrol). By the end of the decade, petrol was about five shillings a gallon.

Public information films warned children of the dangers of traffic and advised them not to step out behind ice cream vans or buses or between parked cars. The main safety adverts on television featured Tufty the Squirrel (or Tufty Fluffytail). Tufty was the idea of Elsie Mills MBE who created safety stories for The Royal Society for the Prevention of Accidents. Tufty first saw the light of day in 1953 and by 1961, the Tufty Club had been launched for under fives. By the early

1970s, there were over 2 million members and the campaign continued well into the 1980s.

Many cars in the late 1960s had seat belts, but many people didn't wear them and there were no rear seat belts for kids or passengers.

The make-do-and-mend attitude came in handy for people who owned cars. They seemed to break down regularly and often required fixing. Many men learnt how to tinker with their own cars and would fix the brakes, lights or any minor problems. Bigger jobs meant a trip to the local garage, of which there were many. Unlike today, cars were less reliable and also more prone to rust.

Most vehicles on the road were British made although some were imported from Europe. It was unheard of for anyone to have a Japanese car.

Police cars were often Ford Cortinas in blue and white. These patrol cars became known as panda cars. Other popular cars used by the police included Morris Minors, Ford Anglias and, as mentioned earlier, Minis.

Amazingly, cars such as the MG Roadster were used for traffic duties and, in the early 1960s, for patrolling the newly built motorways. All made the familiar 'nee-nah' sound when driving to an emergency. It's a noise that children still imitate today, even though modern sirens sound totally different.

In the 1960s, most people were happy catching the bus. If there was a car in the family, Dad would use it to go to work or it might just be used for special journeys or days out. By the later 1960s, there were more cars about, and days to the seaside in the summer (or anywhere else) would mean sitting in a mile-long traffic jam. Roads were less comprehensive and traffic soon became congested. Often a pedestrian could walk past traffic on a hot day and get to his destination long before a car could.

All buses were double-deckers and all were very well-used by people travelling to work or into town. All buses had a driver and a conductor, and you would take your seat before the conductor came around with his ticket machine, shouting, 'Tickets, please!' The fares weren't very dear, perhaps a couple of pennies. A favourite pastime for children was to ask the conductor for a roll of tickets, which he was quite often happy to give. Sitting upstairs with your mum on the bus was an adventure. Making sure that you could sit by the window seemed great fun. Smoking was still allowed on buses back then, and there would always be some teenagers at the back of the bus, swearing (it seems tame nowadays) and puffing cigarettes. Mums would tell them off by saying things like 'there's kids on board', and that would usually be enough for them to quieten down. Sometimes the conductor would object to rowdy youths and would even throw them off the bus and make them walk home. The seats came in purple leatherette material and were generally vandalised. When you reached your stop, you'd ring the bell and the driver would open the door (sometimes too early). Most people thanked the driver before they got off.

There were many other vehicles on the roads at the time, all of which appealed to children, including fire engines, ambulances and steamrollers. Long journeys travelling on holiday, or for days out at the beach, meant taking your I-Spy books. Motorways were quite empty of traffic, and people doing U-turns wasn't unheard of.

For long journeys, many people drove themselves but many also caught a coach or train. For most of the 1960s, there were still steam trains, although they had run alongside diesel locomotives for many years. The last steam train service ran in Britain on 11 August 1968.

By the end of the 1960s, transport had changed greatly. There were many newer, faster roads together with sleeker, stylish cars and other vehicles. Steam trains had gone forever, as had many railway lines. Far more families now owned a car and were able to travel further afield, both to work and on holiday. Cars were no longer just available to the well-off, and were now available to the masses.

4

Entertainment

Running home from school and having your tea as quickly as possible was what most kids did, especially in the summer, so they could go out and play. Climbing trees, riding bikes, playing on building sites and building dens were popular pastimes for boys. Girls roller-skated, played hopscotch and skipped. Push-along scooters, pogo sticks and spacehoppers were also often seen.

Building sites were generally unlocked and unfenced, so boys could have fun running along walls, shooting tin cans and bottles off them with home-made catapults or generally looking for materials to build a den. Most boys had a den hidden away somewhere, usually in the woods. If there was an empty building site, it was the perfect opportunity to find building materials, and some dens could be quite elaborate.

Re-enacting things that had appeared on the television or in films at the cinema was a popular pastime. Boys would pretend to be cowboys and Indians or soldiers, involving battles between the English and Germans. Playing war games usually started with the chants 'who wants a game of war?' or 'we won the war in 1944', and would continue until enough boys had gathered to play a game. The same process carried on even into the 1970s. Once enough boys had been found, two people would pick up sides, choosing people from the line-up. It wasn't much fun if you were the last boy chosen. Once sides were chosen, everyone would run around pretending to machine-gun each other or pretending to throw hand grenades.

In the later 1960s, the games changed a bit. Kids no longer wanted to be their favourite cowboys but instead chose to be Batman and Robin, Randall and Hopkirk, Captain Scarlet, or one of the many other characters on television at the time. Toys featuring guns, walkie-talkies and badges from the *Man from U.N.C.L.E.* made it all more believable. In the 1960s, it wasn't unusual to see a kid with a toy gun, machine gun or even a knife. Cowboy guns fired caps and looked like toys, but the sort of guns that were carried by television secret agents, such as Napoleon Solo and Ilya Kuryakin, looked little different from the real thing. However, nobody was much bothered and there wasn't the worry about imitation guns as there is today. When Batman was on the television, every boy wanted to be just like him. Some even had their own home-made costumes. Copying Captain Scarlet and Joe 90 was also a popular pastime in the late 1960s although, unlike Captain Scarlet, kids weren't indestructible, and many ended up injuring themselves.

The Cubs or the Scouts were very popular and many boys joined, while the girls joined the Brownies or the Guides. A scout leader would teach boys things like orienteering, birdwatching, how to start a fire and a whole range of other activities. Regular camping trips would include singing songs around a fire. All would-be Scouts would have to learn their 'allegiance to the Queen' speech, and had a uniform complete with shorts, shirt, scarf and woggle. Badges could be earned for different tasks and would be sewn to the sleeves of the scout's shirt.

If there was a nearby park or piece of ground, games of football and cricket would be played, especially in the summer months.

Many boys, with the help of their fathers, would construct their own go-karts, which were made with a plank of wood and four discarded pram wheels. Some used larger bicycle wheels at the back. The wheels at the front were fixed to a moveable cross bar which had a length of rope attached to it to aid steering. Some attached a bit of wood at the side, like a lever, which acted as a brake, while some go-karts ran uncontrollably downhill, until they finally came to a halt or crashed. The great thing about a go-kart was that it could be easily constructed from bits and pieces that nobody wanted.

Parks would be full of children, and playgrounds would include swings, roundabouts, see-saws, a witch's hat, a maypole and a slide. Some parks also had metal climbing frames as well as concrete tunnels, cars and boats. Others had real full-size steam engines left over from another era (complete with asbestos!). There were no worries about health and safety, and the floor of the park was hard concrete. There were many accidents, which included falling off a slide or being hit on the back of the head by a swing but, after a few tears, it was mostly forgotten.

Fishing was popular with boys. Some had more expensive rods bought for them on birthdays or at Christmas; others made their own or used their dad's old heavy wooden rods. If there was a river nearby, a kid could happily spend all day fishing. Quite often what was caught wasn't fit for anything except the local cat but a lot of the fun was in the thrill of catching something.

All children would take out a net and a jam jar to try and catch their own tadpoles. A nearby stream or pond was the ideal place to search, and most boys would have a collection in a jam jar on the kitchen window. Watching tadpoles develop and grow legs was fascinating. Many children returned them to ponds once they had changed into frogs, as feeding them was almost impossible.

Collecting birds' eggs was also a popular pastime with boys. There were far more birds around in the 1960s than there are today, and locating their nests wasn't difficult. Although it sounds cruel nowadays, many boys would take an egg from a nest, take it home and remove the inside so that it was ready to display. This involved pricking each end of the egg with a needle and blowing out the contents. Some boys had large collections of eggs, some in display cases. Of course, today, the practice is totally illegal.

Television programmes about spies and secret agents caused kids to try and copy their heroes. Invisible ink was popular for writing secret messages and was available from the local joke shop, or home versions could be made using lemon juice. The nearest thing to a walkie-talkie was connecting two bean tins together by a length of string. By pulling the string tight, kids were meant to be able to talk to the person at the other end. Children had done it for years, although it never worked very well and it was easier to shout.

Books encouraged outdoor life. Works by Enid Blyton made children want to go outside, build dens, solve mysteries and track down baddies. Other books taught children how to identify various trees, birds and other wildlife. If it had been snowing, identifying bird and animal prints was very exciting. Children certainly knew a lot more about the world around them, and most boys could recognise the paw prints of a fox, badger or stoat, although many times, there were only tracks of the local cat or dog!

Dogs roamed freely through the streets; many had no collars or name tags, and would return home only when it was time to eat. Some dogs would become very well known in an area and would accompany children on adventures in the woods or while building dens, which made everything feel very much like the Famous Five. Of course, any dog seen wandering nowadays would be rounded up and taken to the nearest pound, but in the 1960s they were everywhere.

Insect life also fascinated children. Some boys would collect butterflies, although again, today, the practice seems very cruel. Butterflies would be caught with a net, probably the same one that caught tadpoles, put in a jar until they died and then displayed on a board. Creatures such as ladybirds could sometimes be found in their thousands and would be collected in matchboxes; most of the time they were let go afterwards. Nowadays, it's rare to see one ladybird a year, so it's hard to imagine that there were once so many.

Popular outdoor games played included 'it' (or tag) and British Bulldog. Teams would be picked from whoever wanted to play by counting them one by one and saying:

Eeny, meeny, miny, mo,
Catch a tiger by the toe.

If he screams, let him go,
Eeny, meeny, miny, mo.

The person that it finished on was the one picked.

Children everywhere could be heard playing ring-a-ring o' roses, which was accompanied by the following chant:

Ring-a-ring o' roses,
A pocketful of posies,
Atishoo, Atishoo,
We all fall down!

'What's the time, Mr Wolf?' involved one player playing the part of Mr Wolf. Mr Wolf would stand opposite the other players, facing away from them. The players would then chant 'What's the time, Mr Wolf?' and Mr Wolf would reply with a time. If it was 'three o'clock', the players would take three steps closer. In response to the chant, Mr Wolf could also answer, 'Dinner Time', which would then allow him to try and catch one of the players so that they, in turn, became the new 'Mr Wolf'.

Playing marbles in the summer and conkers in the autumn were also well-loved pastimes, and an adventure was to be had searching for horse chestnuts after school on cold, dark autumn nights.

Naughtier kids would take part in cherry knocking where one would dare the other to knock on someone's door and they would all run off. There was always the fear of someone calling the police but it never seemed to happen.

With more cars, lorries and vans on the road, collecting number plates became a well-liked hobby and many boys would have their own notepads and would write down as many as they could. In the same way, some boys would also record train numbers, although this pastime wasn't so popular.

Astronomy was also popular with boys, and some had their own telescopes to watch the night sky. Television programmes and books by Patrick Moore, along with the space programme always in the news, increased interest in the stars and planets in the night sky. Every boy could find the Plough, more commonly known then as the Big Dipper, which fell in the constellation of Ursa Minor. They also knew the planets, where the North Star was, and various facts about the Moon. Many classrooms had a moon chart on their walls at the time.

As the year came to an end, and the evenings grew darker, outdoor activities involved Halloween in October and Guy Fawkes Night in November. In October, some mothers would carve out turnips (pumpkins were hardly seen back then) which would be lit by candles. Kids would wander the streets with the hope that a passer-by would give them an odd penny or, if they were lucky, a sixpence. Most children made a Guy in the lead-up to Guy Fawkes Night and would sit on street corners with it in the evenings, asking, 'Penny for the guy, mister?' Most did quite well out of it, and the money raised would go towards buying sweets or bangers (a type of firework). The build-up to Guy Fawkes Night also involved finding material, mainly wood, to build the biggest bonfire possible. Boys were very adept at this as they already had the knowledge of where to find scrap material for dens or go-karts. There would be a competition in the area as to who could build the biggest bonfire. At the time, councils weren't so bothered about where bonfires were built and they could be found everywhere. Unfortunately, the day of Bonfire Night always fell within school time and many bonfires were set alight early by unruly kids. If the bonfire lasted until the night of 5 November, families would come out of their houses and all gather around. Some would have fireworks, many of the younger kids would have sparklers and some would cook potatoes and Spanish chestnuts in the embers. The Guy, who had made so much money for its owners several days before, would end up on top of the fire. By the end of the evening, everyone would have had a great time and would return home stinking of smoke.

The Christmas period also brought much outdoor activity, especially on Boxing Day, when everyone would be out, trying their new bikes, roller skates or any of the other exciting things that they'd been given for presents.

The outdoor life was an exciting one for children in the

1960s and by the end of the decade, there probably wasn't a child in the land who hadn't built a den, climbed a tree, helped build a go-kart or generally enjoyed playing outside.

Toys and games during the 1960s were vast and varied. There was a huge range of inventive and appealing toys, many of them fondly remembered. One of the most popular for boys was Palitoy's Action Man.

Action Man was launched in 1966. Palitoy had the licence to copy the incredibly popular GI Joe doll, which was hugely successful in America. The company, which was based in Coalville in Leicestershire, produced the action figure to be sold in Great Britain and Australia. The doll was much sought after by boys and came with a huge range of accessories. The first figures available featured a soldier, sailor and pilot. They came with painted-on hair in either blonde, auburn, brown or black. In the early years, the toys competed with the all-British tommy gun, which was manufactured by Pedigree Toys who also produced the Sindy doll. The tommy gun toy was of a higher quality than Action Man, but by 1968 it could no longer compete and disappeared in the same year. They also came with rafts, tanks and motorbikes. Boys everywhere in the 1960s took their Action Man out to play with them, dropping him from high windows on home-made parachutes or playing mock battles with their friends in their gardens. The toy was extremely popular and lasted into the 1980s, by which time it had moveable eagle eyes, gripping hands and flocked hair. Television adverts at Christmas showed Action Man having great adventures incorporating the many extras that were available. This guaranteed that every boy would want an Action Man and everything that went with him on 25 December. The toy was relaunched by Hasbro in 1993, restyled and with new facial features, but it was never quite the same.

Airfix kits were extremely popular with boys in the 1960s, as were models made by rival manufacturers Revell and Frog. Popular kits featured wartime aeroplanes, battleships and cars. Film tie-ins included a model of James Bond's Aston Martin DB5 as well as a kit featuring Bond fighting the infamous Oddjob from Goldfinger. With the craze for space travel, there were models of Apollo's Saturn 5 rocket, the Lunar Module and the Russian Vostok. With the popularity of Gerry Anderson's television show, *Captain Scarlet*, at the end of the 1960s, a kit featuring the Angel Interceptor was produced. There were also models of famous historical figures, including Henry VIII, the Black Prince, Oliver Cromwell, Julius Caesar, Napoleon Bonaparte, Charles I and Anne Boleyn. Other model figures included a Yeoman of the Guard and a lifeguard trumpeter, as well as smaller military figures. Airfix was founded in 1939 but it wasn't until 1949 that their first kit, a promotional model of a tractor, was produced and sold in Woolworths. In 1954, a plastic model of Sir Francis Drake's ship, the *Golden Hind*, was produced, and proved so successful that a kit featuring the Submarine Spitfire was produced in 1955. In the 1960s, building plastic kits became incredibly popular, and Airfix grew immensely to feature models of classic ships, motorcycles and trains.

Corgi Toys first appeared in the UK in 1956. Some of their bestselling cars appeared in the 1960s, including James Bond's Aston Martin DB5, the Batmobile, and the classic car from *Chitty Chitty Bang Bang*. James Bond's DB5 remains their bestselling toy car ever. All cars and vehicles from Corgi sold worldwide. Overseas, a popular car was Black Beauty, which was from *The Green Hornet*. The programme co-starred Bruce Lee but wasn't shown in the UK because it was considered too violent. Corgi Toys were produced by Mettoy, who had been trading since 1933 and had previously mainly produced tinplate. Corgi produced a range of vehicles including popular cars, lorries, vans and tractors, etc. Their most popular vehicles were ones relating to film and television and these included the jeep from *Daktari* (featuring Judy the chimp and Clarence the cross-eyed lion), the Monkeemobile and the Yellow Submarine from the Beatles film of the same name. Vehicles relating to children's programmes included Noddy's car and a train, car and trike from the *Magic Roundabout*, as well as Basil Brush's car.

Dinky cars were rivals to Corgi but generally, their cars were bigger and more expensive. Some of their most popular vehicles were television tie-ins. These included Lady Penelope's pink Rolls-Royce from *Thunderbirds*; the Spectrum Patrol Car, the Spectrum Pursuit Vehicle and the Maximum Security Vehicle from *Captain Scarlet and the Mysterons*; and Sam's car from *Joe 90*. All these vehicles tied in with Gerry Anderson series that were hugely successful at the time. Dinky also produced a large range of very popular everyday cars and vehicles.

Etch a Sketch was introduced in 1960 and allowed children to draw on a screen by turning two dials at the bottom to create pictures. By turning the screen upside down and shaking it, the picture would disappear and then another drawing could be created. The product was hugely successful and was sold worldwide.

Lego had been a hugely successful toy for children for many years. The interlocking bricks were first sold in 1949 and, since then, over 560 billion Lego parts have been produced. Lego allowed children to build whatever they wanted, including cars, trains, and castles, etc. Sets were released featuring a variety of themes including Vikings, dinosaurs, undersea exploration, and many more. A Lego set fuelled a child's imagination and allowed them to build whatever they wanted. Over the years, the sets have become more advanced and include various characters as well as motors, switches and cameras.

Matchbox cars were first introduced in 1953. They were so named because they came in boxes similar to those that contained matches. Matchbox was a brand produced by Lesney, which was founded by Jack Odell, Leslie Smith and Rodney Smith. A model of Queen Elizabeth II's Coronation Coach became Lesney's first toy to sell more than a million. The first Matchbox product was designed by Jack Odell. Odell's daughter attended a school which would only allow children to bring in toys small enough to fit in a matchbox. Odell scaled down Lesney's red-and-green road roller and the toy became the prototype for Matchbox's first 1:75 vehicle. Soon, it was joined by a dumper truck and cement mixer and the three toys became the beginning of the Matchbox range. Other models were soon added to the range, including cars such as the Ford Zodiac, MG Midget and Vauxhall

Cresta. At first, all models were based on British cars, but as the company grew, European and American cars were also included. Their reasonable prices meant that most boys in the 1960s had a collection of Matchbox cars.

Frank Hornby came up with the idea for Meccano back in 1901 and had called it 'Mechanics Made Easy'. The toy consisted of small metal strips with holes, plates, pulleys, gears, and nuts and bolts. The toy was seen as educational as well as fun but very soon demand started to exceed supply so Hornby set up a factory in Liverpool to cope with the additional manufacturing needs. The kits became more and more popular and were soon on sale around the world. By 1907 Hornby had registered the name Meccano, and seven years later an additional factory was opened in Liverpool to keep up with demand. By the 1950s, Meccano was a well-loved toy but, because of the Second World War, production was interrupted when the factory at Binns Road in Liverpool was used to help the war effort. The Korean War in 1950 also disrupted production because of metal shortages but, by the mid-1950s, production was back to normal. Children loved playing with Meccano in the 1960s, and what they constructed was limited only by their imagination. Cranes were a popular item to construct, as were cars, boats and aeroplanes.

Bob Pelham first started making marionettes during the late 1940s. His company had previously been known as Wonky Toys but it became Pelham's Puppets in October 1948. In 1953, the company secured the rights from Disney to manufacture one of their best-loved puppets, Pinocchio. String puppets became very popular during the 1960s, especially with shows made by Gerry Anderson being shown regularly on the television. Other well-loved puppets bought during the time included Huckleberry Hound as well as puppets of pirates, clowns, royalty and animals. Pelham also made a range of glove puppets.

Jack Rosenthal were responsible for making a large range of toys relating to the television series *Thunderbirds*. These were much sought after by boys, and thousands were given by parents as birthday and Christmas presents. The range included the space vehicles that featured in the show: Thunderbird 1, Thunderbird 2, Thunderbird 3, Thunderbird 4 and Thunderbird 5. There was also a version of Lady Penelope's pink Rolls-Royce (FAB 1) as well as Thunderbirds cap guns, water pistols and 3D painting sets. Lady Penelope merchandise included a jewellery set, a dressing table set and a tea set.

Roller skates were well liked by both boys and girls, although girls were more often seen skating along the pavements outside people's houses. The metal roller skates were adjustable in the middle so that they could fit any shoe size.

Scalextric was sought after by every boy. Television and adverts in comics and magazines made the racing track and cars look like something from Le Mans. With dual controls, boys were able to race their cars around the track at speed while trying their best to beat their opponent. The race usually ended with one car, or both, spinning off the track. Scalextric were popular also at amusement arcades and holiday camps, but there was a great thrill in having one of your own and being able to race a range of sleek sports cars at home.

Slinky was a huge coiled spring that became very popular after a television advertising campaign. It suddenly became the toy to have. Its main feature was that it could walk downstairs on its own, which, at the time, seemed amazing. However, although very popular, it was soon discovered that it did little else. Most Slinkys eventually ended up twisted and unusable. A smaller version called Springy was later released but was never as popular as the original.

Spacehoppers seemed fantastic things that you could sit on and bounce all around on in your front room and garden. Television adverts made them look incredible and able to bounce great heights. In reality, it was hard to get them to bounce a few inches off the ground, but they were still great fun. Some kids would even have races on them, which would only end when a spacehopper caught something sharp and ended up punctured.

Spirograph was first sold in 1965 by Denys Fisher and allowed you to make weird and wonderful colourful patterns on a sheet of paper. It consisted of plastic rings with gear teeth. Holes in the rings allowed pens to be used to make a variety of geometric shapes with fantastic results. It sounds very basic nowadays but kept children amused for hours.

Subbuteo, the tabletop football game, was originally sold in the late 1940s but became immensely popular in the 1960s. Competitors flicked their players to score goals. Teams were available in a variety of football strips and the set included many accessories, such as linesmen, stands and crowds, and eventually even a streaker.

Timpo made a vast range of toy soldiers that proved immensely popular with boys. The small plastic figures also included knights, Romans and even Eskimos. Cowboys were very popular in the 1960s and every boy had his own collection and accessories, which included wagons, horses and canoes. Today, they are much sought after by collectors.

Tin robots were hugely popular in the 1960s. Most were made in Japan, where a huge range of tin space toys were created after the war. Robots could walk, talk, show mock-television in their chests and fire guns. They were quite advanced for their time, and have since become very collectable. Some were made in factories that reused tin from drink cans as could be seen when they were taken apart. Other tin toys from Japan included spaceships, cars, lorries and aeroplanes.

Viewmaster was a plastic viewer that allowed its owner to view, in 3D, round cardboard wheels that featured transparencies covering a range of subjects. Many were educational and showed places at home and around the world. There were others that featured popular television shows such as *Top Cat*, *Star Trek* and *William Tell*.

There were endless board games produced in the 1960s and all were extremely popular. New ones would come out every year, just in time for Christmas.

The Archers board game was produced by Chad Valley and was based on the popular BBC radio series. Each player had his own farm and had to collect livestock along the way. The winner was the first person to complete their farm.

Ask Me Another was produced by J. & L. Randall in

1965 and involved three players. It was based on the popular television show. Contestants had to roll a dice, and whichever square they landed on had a general knowledge question of varying difficulty.

Batman and Robin was based on the television show featuring Adam West and Burt Ward. The first player to get around the track and arrive safely in the Batcave won the game.

Battle of the Little Big Horn was released by Waddington's in 1963 and featured Sioux and Cheyenne Indians battling against the US Cavalry. The aim of the game was to get General Custer's flag clear of the battlefield.

Beetle was hugely popular in the 1960s and involved players rolling a dice with the aim of being the first to construct a plastic beetle. The game had been around in various forms since 1927.

Blast-Off! cashed in on the craze for anything to do with space after the successful Apollo moon landing. It was produced in 1969 by Waddington's. It involved the player blasting off from earth and visiting the moon and nine planets before returning home.

Bonanza was released by Parker Brothers in 1964 and featured the characters from the popular television series. The aim was to reach the Ponderosa, with four cowboys, as quickly as possible.

Chess, still as popular today, was seen as a game of skill and patience. There were undoubtedly many games of chess played in the 1960s, although younger children might have considered it too highbrow and boring. Draughts was a much more fun game for kids.

Cluedo was produced by Waddington's and was first available in 1949. The game featured six characters: Miss Scarlett, Colonel Mustard, Mrs White, Reverend Green, Mrs Peacock and Professor Plum. The aim of the game was to get around the board, which included several different rooms of a mansion, collecting clues while trying to deduce who murdered the game's victim, Dr Black. The idea for the game was devised by Anthony E. Pratt, who was a solicitor's clerk from Birmingham.

Contraband was first released in 1950 but was hugely successful throughout the 1960s. One player took the part of the customs officer while the others played travellers who lie or tell the truth about any contraband they carry.

Dizzy Bug was manufactured by Whitman in 1968. The aim of the game was to get the bug into one of the many coloured holes on the board to score points.

Electric Derby was made by J. & L. Randall Ltd in 1964. It featured five horses which were propelled down the track by a ball bearing. Players would bet on which horse they thought would win.

Escalado was a horse racing game which was patented by a Swiss inventor called Arthur Gueydan in 1928. It featured six mechanical horses and, like Electric Derby, players would try to predict which one was going to win.

Everest was first released in 1961 and players had to guide their three climbers up the mountain. The winner was the first player to get one of his climbers to the summit.

Flutter, a stock exchange game, was made by Spear's games and first came out in 1950. Players started with £300 and could win the game by buying and selling shares whose value was decided by a roll of the dice.

Formula 1 first appeared on the market in 1962. It was a simple racing game where each player had his own dashboard which came complete with a speedometer. Formula 1 was very popular in the 1960s, at a time when drivers commanded celebrity status. The game appealed very much to boys.

Frustration was one of the most popular games of the 1960s. It featured a pop-o-matic dice roller. Each player got his or her own coloured pawns, and each pawn had to travel around the board to win the game. The winner was the player with all their pawns on the finish lane.

Ker-Plunk was the hit of the year when it first came out in 1967. It was produced by MB Games and featured a tube with intercrossing sticks with marbles above them. The aim of the game was to pull out the sticks without the marbles falling. Any marbles that fell were kept by the player who pulled out the stick. Once the last marble had fallen, players counted how many marbles they had and the winner was the player with the least.

Magic Robot consisted of a tiny robot with a pointer that was placed at the centre of the board. The game featured questions and, by using a series of magnets, the robot, once spun, was able to point to the correct answer.

Misfits was made by Spear's Games and came out in 1964. It included sixty cards with the hat, face, body and legs of a particular character. The aim of the game was to create five full characters.

Monopoly was created in 1934 although the idea for it went back much further. It was an incredibly well-liked board game in the 1960s, usually played by four members of the same family or with several friends. The board, counters and houses have become iconic over the years and are instantly recognisable nowadays. The counters included a Scottie dog, a ship, an iron, a book, a top hat, a racing car and a thimble. The idea was to make your way around the board, collecting £200 when you passed go, while buying property along the way. The winner was the person who ended up with all of the money.

Mouse Trap was probably one of the best and most original of all the board games released in the 1960s. It featured an elaborate mouse trap, which was built up piece by piece by rolling a dice and proceeding around the board. The aim was to capture the opponent's mouse under the trap at the end.

Risk! originally came out in the late 1950s but was just as popular in the 1960s. It was a war game where each player had an army unit which was used to attack his opponent on the roll of a dice.

Scrabble was very popular in the 1960s and is still played today. A variation of the game had been around since the 1930s. The game began to be sold in the UK in 1955 and was manufactured by J. W. Spear's. The game involved spelling out words on a grid using tiles with individual letters on them. Each tile carried its own point score and the winner was the person who had the highest score at the end of the game.

Snakes and Ladders involved rolling a dice to proceed to

the top of the board. If a player landed on a ladder he could go up it, but if he landed on a snake he had to go down. The game originally came from India, where it was known as Moksha Patam, but it eventually made its way to England. Milton Bradley later produced a similar game in America called Chutes and Ladders.

Spy Ring was made by Waddington's in 1965 and players played a spy and his contact, with the aim of collecting as many secrets as they could. The player who collected the most valuable secrets was the winner.

Table Soccer was released by Waddington's in 1965 and was a game of dexterity. Each game contained blue and red players, the game board, with goals for each end, and white scoring discs.

Tiddlywinks featured small coloured plastic discs which had to be flipped using another disc into a pot. The game was considered a child's game, but in 1955, the University of Cambridge introduced an adult game using tiddlywinks with more complex rules, strategy and competition. However, no family playing the game in their house in the 1960s would have been concerned by that; it was just a bit of fun!

Tippet was a balancing game using plastic counters which had to be placed on a plastic contraption, similar to a roundabout, without causing it to tip over. The winner was the person at the end who had the most counters.

Today, it's hard to imagine the great popularity that board games once had. In a time when there were no computers or other modern devices, and when television channels were few, board games were great entertainment for both families and friends.

Most families in the 1960s rented their televisions from outlets such as DER for a cost of twenty-five to thirty shillings a month. Early models were tabletop appliances with 12- to 17-inch screens. All had wooden surrounds and the more modern models came with their own thin 1960s-type legs. Once you'd chosen the model that you wanted, it would be delivered to your home and a technician would set it up. To many people, television was a relatively new thing which had only really taken off with the Coronation of Queen Elizabeth II in 1953. Televisions had appealing model names such as Starmaster, the Consolette and the Major. All had to be tuned in manually between channels.

Watching the television was a family event, and everyone would gather in their front room to watch their favourite programmes. At the beginning of the decade, popular programmes included new shows such as *Young at Heart*, a music programme; *Police Surgeon*, starring Ian Hendry as Dr Geoffrey Brent; *Dangerman*, with Patrick MacGoohan as secret agent John Drake; and *Coronation Street*.

Quiz shows were very popular, and two of the favourites were *Take Your Pick* with Michael Miles and *Double Your Money* with Hughie Green. *Take Your Pick* had started its television life in 1955, when ITV was first set up, and continued until 1968. It had previously been broadcast on *Radio Luxembourg* in the early 1950s. *Double Your Money* also started out life on *Radio Luxembourg* and moved to ITV in 1955. It became one of the most consistently popular shows on ITV until it ended in 1968. The format of the show involved questions being asked and the prize money doubling every time there was a correct answer, up to a total of £1,000. One of Green's most popular assistants on the show was Monica Rose who had been a accounts clerk before appearing on the show as a contestant. She also joined Green on his next successful quiz show, *The Sky's the Limit*.

Shows for small children, many of which had been made in the 1950s, included *Andy Pandy*, *The Flower Pot Men*, and *Rag, Tag and Bobtail*. *Andy Pandy* had started life on the BBC in 1952 as part of the *Watch with Mother* series, and was hugely popular throughout the 1960s, as were Bill and Ben, *The Flower Pot Men*.

By 1965, a new show was made, *Camberwick Green*, to replace *Andy Pandy* but there was an outcry and both shows continued to be shown. *Camberwick Green* included narration and song vocals by Brian Cant. Each episode would begin with a rotating music box featuring one of the characters from the show. The opening narration would announce, 'Here is a box, a musical box, wound up and ready to play. But this box can hide a secret inside. Can you guess what is in it today?' Popular characters included Police Constable McGarry, Mickey Murphy the baker, Dr Mopp (complete with vintage car), Mrs Honeyman (the town gossip), Windy Miller, Jonathan Bell and Mr Dagenham, a travelling salesman. Nearby was Pippin Fort, a military establishment run by Captain Snort and Sergeant-Major Grout. The short programme was immensely popular with children and led on to the hugely successful *Trumpton* in 1967, which again was narrated by Brian Cant.

Every episode of *Trumpton* would start with a shot of the town clock and the words 'telling the time, steadily, sensibly; never too quickly, never too slowly. Telling the time for Trumpton.' Characters included in the show included the mayor, Mr Troop the town clerk, Chippy Minton the carpenter with his apprentice son Nibbs, Mr Platt the clockmaker, Mrs Cobbit the florist and Miss Lovelace the milliner, together with her Pekinese dogs called Mitzi, Daphne and Lulu. Perhaps the most remembered characters are the men of the nearby fire station, who would be mentioned in every show by Captain Flack reciting at roll call: 'Pugh Pugh, Barney McGrew, Cuthbert, Dibble, Grub.'

The most successful maker of children's shows on British television in the 1960s was Gerry Anderson, whose most popular programmes included *Fireball XL5* (1962–63), *Stingray* (1964–65), *Thunderbirds* (1965–66), *Captain Scarlet and the Mysterous* (1967–68) and *Joe 90* (1968–69). All featured 'Supermarionation' using modified puppets, complete with strings. *Torchy the Battery Boy* told the story of a doll, powered by a battery, who had a light in his head. *Supercar* featured a car, invented by Rudolph Popkiss and Horatio Beaker, which was capable of vertical take-off. It was piloted by Mike Mercury, who was voiced by Canadian actor, Graydon Gould. In the first episode, the crew of *Supercar* rescued passengers from a crashed plane. Two of the passengers were Jimmy Gibson and his pet monkey, Mitch, who later appeared in following episodes of *Supercar*.

Fireball XL5 is very fondly remembered, and featured the space missions of Colonel Steve Zodiac of the World Space Patrol. Thirty-nine half-hour black-and-white episodes were made, all shot on 35 mm film. The show was set in the year 2062 and other members of the crew included Doctor Venus, Professor Matthew Matic and robot co-pilot Robert. The characters were voiced by Paul Maxwell, Sylvia Anderson, David Graham and John Bluthal. The show was hugely popular and led to a range of merchandise, including model kits, puppets and ray guns. Comic strips and annuals also appeared, and proved very popular.

Stingray, made between 1964 and 1965, became the first Gerry Anderson 'Supermarionation' production to be filmed in colour. American television was preparing to broadcast in colour, although Great Britain didn't begin transmitting in colour until November 1969. The show revolved around the crew of a submarine that belonged to the World Aquanaut Security Patrol (WASP). The main characters included Captain Troy Tempest (whose look was based on the actor James Garner) and Lieutenant George Lee 'Phones' Sheridan who piloted the submarine. They received their orders from Commander Samuel Shore, whose daughter, Lieutenant Atlanta Shore, has a soft spot for Troy. Each week, the crew of *Stingray* encountered various undersea enemies including The Aquaphibians, who were commanded by King Titan (based on Laurence Olivier). It was hugely successful and again led to a large range of merchandise.

Thunderbirds first appeared on ITV in 1965, and became Gerry Anderson's most successful show. It told the story of International Rescue, a top-secret organisation that operated from Tracy Island in the South Pacific Seas. Jeff Tracy, a retired, widowed multimillionaire, and his five sons operated the Thunderbirds fleet. Tracy's sons were Scott, Virgil, Alan, Gordon and John Tracy, who were all named after Mercury Seven astronauts. Other regular characters included Brains, a scientist and engineer; Kyrano, the Tracys' Malaysian manservant; Tin-Tin, Kyrano's daughter; and Grandma Tracy. Their arch-enemy was The Hood, who operated from a temple in the Malaysian jungle. The show also featured the undercover agent Lady Penelope Creighton-Ward and her butler and chauffeur, Aloysius 'Nosey' Parker. The vehicles featured in the show became much sought after by children. The need to keep up with the demand for Thunderbird 1, 2, 3, 4 and 5 toys meant that AP Films Merchandising issued 120 licences to manufacture products and even bought a toy company, J. Rosenthal. Of all the vehicles featured in the show, Thunderbird 2, which incorporated Thunderbird 4, became the most popular. For a while, the Thunderbirds characters appeared everywhere – on cereal, in books, and on badges. By the end of 1966, the show was so popular that the shopping season was nicknamed *Thunderbirds Christmas* because of all the merchandise that was sold.

Gerry Anderson's next production in 1967 was *Captain Scarlet and the Mysterons*. The show was set in 2068 and featured Captain Scarlet, who formed part of a worldwide security organisation known as Spectrum. Scarlet defended the world against the Mysterons, who were a race of Martians who had declared war on Earth. Each week they would appear as two lit circles accompanied by a deep voice announcing, 'We are the Mysterons!' Captain Scarlet acquired the Mysterons' healing power, known as retrometabolism, which made him indestructible. He was accompanied in his adventures by Captain Blue, Captain Black (who had fallen under the powers of the Mysterons), Captain Ochre, Captain Magenta and Captain Grey, who all came under the command of Lieutenant Green and Colonel White. Captain Scarlet was voiced by Francis Matthews, who was chosen because he sounded like Cary Grant. Captain Blue was voiced by Ed Bishop, who would later go on to star in Gerry Anderson's live-action production *UFO*. Also featured in the show were the female pilots of the Spectrum Angel fighter squadron, including Destiny Angel, Symphony Angel, Rhapsody Angel, Melody Angel and Harmony Angel. The production again spawned a vast array of merchandise, which was popular with children everywhere. For a while, there wasn't a boy in Great Britain who didn't want to be

Captain Scarlet, and bubblegum cards were swapped in every school playground.

Gerry Anderson's next production was *Joe 90* in 1968. *Joe 90* featured the adventures of a nine-year-old boy who led a double life as a spy after an invention by his scientist father that allowed him to absorb knowledge and skills from the top academic and military minds. Working for WIN (World Intelligence Network), Joe aimed for world peace while saving lives. The show was incredibly popular and during 1968, there wasn't a nine-year-old boy in the school playground who didn't think he had the powers of *Joe 90*. Joe 90's face greeted every boy at breakfast time on the box of Kellogg's Sugar Smacks, replacing Thunderbirds and Captain Scarlet.

Gerry Anderson's last production of the 1960s was *The Secret Service*, which again featured Supermarionation. It told of the adventures of Father Stanley Unwin but was nowhere near as popular as Anderson's previous productions during the 1960s, and, today, it is mostly forgotten.

In 1963, it was hard to imagine the effect that a new science fiction show would have on the population of Great Britain. *Dr Who* was first broadcast on BBC One at 5.15 p.m. on Saturday 23 November 1963. William Hartnell, an actor made famous on television in the 1950s and early 1960s in the *Army Game*, was chosen to play the Doctor. It was a part that he was uncertain about, but it was to become his best-remembered role. The remit for the show was 'no bug-eyed monsters', but an appearance by the Daleks changed all this. Children loved the show. It gave them nightmares and the phrase 'watching from behind the sofa' entered the English language. The show was huge, and Hartnell was recognised as Dr Who wherever he went. Suffering from ill health, Hartnell left the role in 1966, saying, 'There's only one man in England who can take over, and that's Patrick Troughton.' William Hartnell regenerated into Patrick Troughton in 1966, first appearing in Episode 4, of The Tenth Planet. At first, it was felt that Troughton was too different from Hartnell to successfully carry on the role. However, it soon became clear that everyone loved him in the part and he became every bit as popular as Hartnell had been. The Cybermen were introduced in The Tenth Planet and resulted in the Doctor's regeneration. New monsters in the show included the Yetis, the Ice Warriors and the Krotons. The Master first appeared in The Mind Robber, and there was a welcome return of the Doctor's most famous enemy in The Power of the Daleks (1966) and The Evil of the Daleks (1967). Shouts of 'exterminate!' could be heard in every playground up and down the land. Troughton remained in the role until the end of the 1960s, and was replaced by Jon Pertwee in 1970.

American shows played a huge part of a child's viewing in the 1960s. Some of the best science fiction shows were *Voyage to the Bottom of the Sea* (1964–68), *Lost in Space* (1965–68), and *Land of the Giants* (1968).

Voyage to the Bottom of the Sea featured the adventures of the crew of the *Seaview*, a futuristic nuclear submarine. The main characters included Admiral Harriman Nelson (played by Richard Basehart) and the submarine's designer and commander, Lee Crane (David Hedison). Regular crew members included Lieutenant Commander Chip Morton (Bob Dowdell), Chief Sharkey (Terry Becker), Kowalski (Del Monroe) and Sparks (Arch Whiting). The show was the first of four hugely popular science fiction shows from Irwin Allen. *Voyage to the Bottom of the Sea* featured conflict with hostile foreign governments as well as sea creatures, monsters and aliens. It ran for 110 episodes before ending in 1968.

Lost in Space featured the adventures of the Robinson family, who were marooned in space because of the actions of the onboard psychologist and foreign spy, Dr Zachary Smith (played by Jonathan Harris). The show is set in 1997 on board the *Jupiter 2* on a five-and-a-half-year journey to a planet orbiting the star Alpha Centauri. Due to Dr Smith's sabotage, the *Jupiter 2* becomes lost in space. On board are Professor John Robinson (played by Guy Williams, of Zorro fame), his wife Maureen (played by June Lockhart), and their children, Judy (Marta Kristen), Penny (Angela Cartwright) and Will (Billy Mumy). They are accompanied by their pilot, US Space Corps Major Donald West (Mark Goddard), and a robot (Bob May). The show featured many monsters but the best episodes revolved around Dr Smith, Will Robinson and the Robot, whose many catchphrases included 'Danger, Will Robinson! Danger!' and 'Warning! Warning! Alien approaching!' Dr Smith also had his own catchphrases, such as 'Oh, the pain, the pain!' and 'Silence, you ninny!'

The Time Tunnel (1966–67) featured Dr Douglas Phillips (Robert Colbert) and Dr Anthony Newman (James Darren) as two time travellers who found themselves in a range of situations, stuck in time, unable to return home. Anthony Newman originally enters the Time Tunnel after a threat to withdraw funding for the government venture, code-named Project Tic-Toc. His aim is to prove that a man can be sent back in time and return home safely. However, when he gets stuck in time, Dr Douglas Phillips follows him into the tunnel and tries to rescue him. Their first adventure takes place onboard the *Titanic* and shows the duo desperately trying to warn people of the impending doom that awaits them. Trying to bring them back to the present day and controlling the tunnel are Lieutenant General Heywood Kirk (Whit Bissell) assisted by Dr Raymond Swain (John Zaremba) and Dr Ann MacGregor (Lee Meriwether). Each week, at the end of the episode, they found themselves transported to another place in time, unable to get home. The show ran for thirty episodes, but rather than returning home in the final episode, they found themselves back on the *Titanic*, starting the journey all over again. Each week the show would start with the words:

> Two American scientists are lost in the swirling maze of past and future ages, during the first experiments on America's greatest and most secret project, the Time Tunnel. Tony Newman and Doug Phillips now tumble helplessly toward a new fantastic adventure, somewhere along the infinite corridors of time.

Like most sci-fi shows of the time, it had a very memorable theme tune.

Star Trek ran from 1966 to 1969 and featured the crew of the Starship *Enterprise*, exploring space in the twenty-third century, whose aim was stated every week at the beginning of the show: 'Space: the final frontier. These are the voyages of the Starship *Enterprise*. Its five-year mission: to explore strange new worlds, to seek out new life and new civilisations, to boldly go where no man has gone before.' The show featured Captain James T. Kirk (William Shatner), Spock (Leonard Nimoy), Dr Leonard 'Bones' McCoy (DeForest Kelley), Montgomery 'Scotty' Scott (James Doohan), Uhura (Nichelle Nichols), Hikaru Sulu (George Takei) and Pavel Chekov (Walter Koenig). Each week, the crew battled with strange beings from other worlds, most notably the Klingons and the Romulans. The show was hugely successful and resulted in many spin-off series and movies.

Land of the Giants was Irwin Allen's fourth and final sci-fi series of the 1960s. It followed the crew and passengers of the *Spindrift* en route from Los Angeles to London. The programme, which was first shown in 1968, was set in the future in the year 1983. After hitting a space storm, the occupants are transported to a strange planet where everyone else is giant, and rewards are offered by the government for the capture of 'little people'. The show ran for fifty-one hour-long episodes and was shot entirely in colour. The aim of the crew was to repair their craft and to return to Earth. However, by the end of the series in 1969, they were still stuck on the Land of the Giants. The show featured many actors who were well known from other programmes during the 1960s, including Gary Conway (Captain Steve Burton), Don Marshall (Dan Erickson), Don Matheson (Mark Wilson), Kurt Kaszner (Alexander Fitzhugh), Stefan Arngrim (Barry Lockridge), Deanna Lund (Valerie Scott), Heather Young (Betty Hamilton) and Kevin Hagen (Inspector Kobick).

During 1966, musical comedy was provided by *The Monkees*, who for a while, were bigger than The Beatles and were mobbed wherever they went.

Well-loved American comedies included *The Beverly Hillbillies* (1962–71), *Hogan's Heroes* (1965), and *Green Acres* (1965–71), but there were many more. Favourite British comedies included *Steptoe and Son* (1962–65, famous for the catchphrase 'You dirty old man'), *Till Death Do Us*

Part (1965), and *Monty Python's Flying Circus* (1969–74). *Please Sir!* was loved by schoolchildren, who could associate with the programme, although most of the 'children' featured seemed to be about twenty-six! Police and detective series included *No Hiding Place* (1959–67) with Johnny Briggs; *Gideon's Way* (1965–66) starring John Gregson, and *Hadleigh* (1969–76). Westerns were also very popular, and some of the best were *Sugarfoot, Bonanza*, and *High Chaparral*. Dramas featuring animals were many, and included *Flipper* (1964–67), *Skippy the Bush Kangaroo* (1966–68), and *Gentle Ben* (1967–69). Older shows such as *Rin Tin Tin* and *Champion the Wonder Horse* were repeated often. Cartoons featured on the television all the time. Early ones included *Popeye the Sailor* (1960), *Secret Squirrel* (1965–66), and *The Pink Panther Show* (1969–79). Back in Britain, popular series included *Danger Man* (1960–62), *Adam Adamant Lives!* (1966–67), and *Randall and Hopkirk* (1969). Well-loved soaps included *Coronation Street* (1960–present), *Dr Finlay's Casebook* (1962–71) and *The Newcomers* (1965–69). Acts like Morecambe and Wise, Tommy Cooper and Arthur Askey all appeared on television regularly, while music shows featured Cilla Black, Tom Jones and Val Doonican.

The Sky at Night was first shown in 1957, and its presenter, Patrick Moore, through his books and television appearances, increased awareness of and interest in the surrounding solar system. Many young boys got into astronomy purely because of Patrick Moore, and many had binoculars and telescopes so that they could study the planets and stars.

Children's shows included *Animal Magic* with Johnny Morris, *The Magic Roundabout* (1964–71) and *The Flaxton Boys* (1969–73).

Animal Magic (1962–83) featured Johnny Morris as a zookeeper at Bristol Zoo. The great attraction of the show was that Morris would do all the voices of the animals. His co-presenters over the years included Gerald Durrell, Tony Soper, Keith Shackleton, David Taylor and Terry Nutkins.

Blue Peter first aired in 1958, although the 1960s team is probably the best remembered, and included John Noakes,

Valerie Singleton and Peter Purves. Together, they travelled to foreign lands, showed children how to make gifts and Christmas decorations (using sticky-back plastic), and hosted a range of guests, the most memorable being Lulu the elephant. The show was loved by children everywhere, and pleased their parents because it was seen to be educational.

Crackerjack first appeared on television in 1955 and continued until 1984. The show was introduced by the phrase 'It's Friday, it's five o'clock ... It's *Crackerjack!*' During the 1960s, it was hosted by Leslie Crowther, and later by Michael Aspel. Both presenters were incredibly popular with children. The show consisted of games (with prizes), a comedy double act, music, and a short comedy play at the end. The comedy act Don and Pete (Don Maclean and Peter Glaze) are fondly remembered.

Orlando (1965–68) was much loved by children during the 1960s, although it's almost forgotten today. Cut-outs of the characters featured on the backs of Kellogg's Cornflake packets. Sam Kydd, a veteran of many British movies, played the lead character, Orlando O'Connor. The thriller, which included tales of espionage, ran for seventy-nine episodes over four series. The character of O'Connor had originally appeared in the adult adventure series *Crane*, which starred Patrick Allen. Many children preferred action series that were meant for adults, and the spin-off show was a reaction to that.

Freewheelers (1968–73) was made after its creator, Chris McMaster, saw how popular shows such as *The Avengers* were with children and decided to make a show aimed at a younger audience. The show revolved around three youths and their adventures, which involved spying and espionage. They answered to Colonel Buchan (played by Ronald Leigh-Hunt), and the show featured fast paced action and high-tech gadgets. Memorable cast members included Wendy Padbury (formerly in *Dr Who*), Chris Chittell and Adrian Wright.

The Flaxton Boys (1969–73) was set in the West Riding of Yorkshire and the stories, over four series, covered the years 1854 to 1945. It was set at Flaxton Hall and featured the adventures of different generations of boys, usually a member of the Flaxton family and his best friend. The stories contained all the things that a boy found interesting in the 1960s, including searching for hidden treasure, solving cryptic clues, ghostly apparitions and the odd villain and spy thrown in for good measure. It was great stuff and every boy at the time watched it.

On a Sunday afternoon in 1969, *The Flaxton Boys* would always be followed by *The Golden Shot*, and the nagging thought in the back of every child's mind was that there was school the next day!

The Eurovision Song Contest was a huge event in the 1960s, attracting millions of viewers. Great Britain won the contest in 1967, with 'Puppet on a String' sung by Sandie Shaw. Britain was also one of the four joint winners in 1969, with 'Boom Bang-a-Bang', sung by Lulu.

Sport played a big part in television viewing during the 1960s, with the biggest event being the World Cup in 1966. Never has a match been so cheered and so watched by the British public. The vision of Bobby Moore being raised on to his teammates' shoulders while holding the World Cup, as well as the immortal words 'some people are on the pitch! They think it's all over! It is now!', will forever remain in the minds of anyone who saw it at the time, and it is still seen as England's biggest sporting achievement. Wrestling was on the television as part of *World of Sport* on Saturday at 4 p.m. It was so popular that streets and shops would empty as people rushed home to watch it. Favourite wrestlers of the time included Les Kellett, Mick McManus and Jackie Pallo.

There were so many fantastic television shows during the 1960s that it would take another book to mention them all. Even the adverts between the programmes on ITV were much enjoyed, and the best of these included the PG Chimps, Nimble and Cadbury's Fruit and Nut.

The following is a typical BBC Saturday viewing in 1968:

10.00 a.m. *Developing a Small Firm*
10.30 a.m. *Suivez la Piste* (which only went on to 11.00 a.m. and then there was a gap in transmission)

12.00 p.m. *The Weather Man*
12.05 p.m. *Laurel and Hardy*
12.25 p.m. *ZOKKO!*
12.45 p.m. *Grandstand* which included:
   12.55 p.m. Fight of the Week
   1.20 p.m. Football Preview
   1.30 p.m. Professional Tennis
   1.50 p.m. Racing
   2.05 p.m. Amateur Boxing
   2.20 p.m. Racing
   2.35 p.m. Amateur Boxing
   2.50 p.m. Racing
   3.10 p.m. Rugby League
   3.25 p.m. Ice Hockey
   3.45 p.m. Rugby League
   4.25 p.m. Ice Hockey
   4.40 p.m. Teleprinter
   4.46 p.m. Ice Hockey
   4.55 p.m. Results Service
5.15 p.m. *Dr Who*
5.40 p.m. The news
5.50 p.m. *Tom and Jerry*

A trip to the cinema in the 1960s was a treat, and most film houses would show two major films together with cartoons in between, often featuring Bugs Bunny or the Road Runner. This went down well even with adults. Blockbusters such as *Goldfinger* would cause huge queues around the cinema. A manager or commissionaire would make sure that there was no trouble in the queue and that everyone was of the right age to see the film (many children would try sneaking in), and ensured that everything ran smoothly.

Although most homes now had their own television set, nearly all were still quite small and black and white. There was nothing to compare with seeing the latest blockbuster on the big screen in full colour.

For children, most cinemas had their own Saturday-morning picture club. There would be a main feature, usually an action/adventure-type film, together with a weekly serial and cartoons. The clubs mainly appealed to boys, and there would often be chaos in the cinema as they climbed over the seats to get to each other either to fight or to re-enact something that was going on in the film.

The James Bond series of films, including *Dr No* (1962), *Goldfinger* (1964), *Thunderball* (1965), *You Only Live Twice* (1967) and *On Her Majesty's Secret Service* (1969), were hugely popular with boys, although, technically, many shouldn't have been allowed to see the movies because of the age restriction. *Goldfinger*, starring Sean Connery, featured the villains Auric Goldfinger and his manservant Odd Job. Another 'star' of the film was Bond's Aston Martin DB5, which came complete with machine guns, revolving number plates, a tyre-slicing device and the all-important ejector seat. The huge success of the movie led to Corgi's version of the DB5 becoming one of their bestsellers, and spawned a range of other Bond merchandise, including plastic models and bubblegum cards.

War films still proved to be popular and all fired the imaginations of young boys.

The Guns of Navarone (1961) starred Gregory Peck, David Niven and Anthony Quinn, and told the story of a group of British mercenaries who are sent to occupied Greece with the objective of destroying a massive German gun emplacement.

The Longest Day (1962) told the story of D-Day, both from the Allied and German point of view. It starred John Wayne, Richard Burton and Robert Ryan. The story, told from different aspects of the attack, weaved together and portrayed the event as dramatically as possible, engrossing the audience. Also appearing in the film were Paul Anka, Red Buttons, Eddie Albert, Sean Connery, Fabian and Henry Fonda, as well as a host of other well-known stars of the day.

The Dirty Dozen (1967) featured Lee Marvin, Ernest Borgnine, Charles Bronson, Telly Savalas and a host of other stars. Marvin played Major Reisman, whose job it was to recruit and train twelve convicted murderers. The aim was to land them in Europe so that they could assassinate Hitler's

German officers on the eve of D-Day. The film was directed by Robert Aldrich.

Where Eagles Dare (1968) starred Richard Burton and Clint Eastwood, who played part of a group of soldiers sent to rescue a US general from a castle held by the SS. The general has knowledge of the D-Day landings and the British decide that none of the information must get into the hands of the Germans no matter what the cost.

Battle of Britain (1969) featured a whole host of stars, including Michael Caine, Trevor Howard, Laurence Olivier, Kenneth More, Michael Redgrave, Ralph Richardson and many, many more. It was rated 'A' when it was released, which meant children had to be accompanied by an adult to see it. However, many just went with their pals, and it was the talk of the playground and much re-enacted. The story concerned the battle over British airspace in 1940 between the Royal Air Force and Germany's Luftwaffe.

The craze for anything to do with space travel increased the interest in science fiction films, and they proved incredibly popular especially with boys.

The Time Machine (1960) starred Rod Taylor as a Victorian time traveller. The story was based on H. G. Wells's novel of 1895. The film was hugely successful and won an Academy Award for best special effects in 1961. The film was produced and directed by George Pal. Taylor plays H. G. Wells, who invents a time machine that allows him to travel into the future. There, he witnesses further wars, and in the year 802,701 encounters warring tribes, the Eloi and the Morlocks. Attacked by the Morlocks, he manages to make his escape in the time machine and return to 1900. His friends scoff at his stories and the film ends with him leaving once more in the time machine. George Pal had planned a sequel to the film but died before it could be made.

The two *Dr Who* movies cashed in on the success of the television series and starred Peter Cushing as the Doctor. Both films included the show's most notorious enemies, the Daleks. In the first movie, the Doctor was accompanied by Roy Castle, Jennie Linden and Roberta Tovey. In the second movie, he was accompanied by Bernard Cribbins, instead of Roy Castle. Bernard Cribbins would later make a reappearance in the television series, appearing opposite David Tennant.

2001: A Space Odyssey (1968) was based on a novel written by Arthur C. Clarke. The film was directed by Stanley Kubrick and starred Keir Dullea. The film featured amazing visual effects as well as a soundtrack of classical music. When it opened, it received mixed reviews, although today it is seen as a cinema classic. The story revolved around the discovery of a mysterious monolith on Earth, which was followed by the discovery of another on the moon, charting man's evolutionary progress. A race begins between computer (HAL) and human (Bowman) to discover further monoliths throughout the solar system. The film was a visual delight but confused many.

Planet of the Apes (1968) is set in a future where apes rule instead of humans. Three astronauts crash on an unknown planet and are soon captured by apes. Two are killed, leaving Taylor (played by Charlton Heston – 'Take your stinkin' paws off me, you damned dirty ape!') to try to reason with the apes. Because he can talk (unlike the other humans on the planet), he is seen as a threat. At the end of the film, he escapes the apes' clutches, and while riding on a horse with his new companion, Nova, he discovers the remains of the Statue of Liberty and realises that he is actually on Earth, although far into the future. The film spawned several sequels, some of which were better than others. These included *Beneath the Planet of the Apes* (1970), *Escape from the Planet of the Apes* (1971), *Conquest of the Planet of the Apes* (1972) and *Battle for the Planet of the Apes* (1973).

Stories of other worlds and strange creatures were very popular, too. *Mysterious Island* (1961) was based on the novel by Jules Verne and told the story of a group of soldiers who escape from an American Civil War camp by hot-air balloon. The balloon takes them across the Pacific Ocean before crashing on a desolate island. There, they find huge creatures, including bees and crabs. The film starred British actor Michael Craig as Captain Cyrus Harding, Joan Greenwood as Lady Mary Fairchild and Herbert Lom as Captain Nemo.

Jason and the Argonauts (1963) starred Todd Armstrong as Jason in his search for the Holy Grail. The most spectacular thing about the film was Ray Harryhausen's stop-motion animation, and particularly remembered are the fighting skeletons. Harryhausen also worked on *Mysterious Island*, *The Three Worlds of Gulliver* (1960) and *The 7th Voyage of Sinbad* (1958), but regarded *Jason and the Argonauts* as his best work. The film looked impressive on the big screen, and Tom Hanks later called the epic 'the greatest movie of all time'.

The Three Worlds of Gulliver captured children's imaginations as they watched the hero of the piece, Dr Lemuel Gulliver (played by Kerwin Mathews), travel the globe encountering little people (Lilliputians) and giants on the island of Brobdingnag. The movie, again, featured stop-motion effects from Ray Harryhausen, including an attack by a giant squirrel.

Musicals remained popular in the 1960s and some of the best were *West Side Story* (1961), *My Fair Lady* (1964), and The Beatles' *Yellow Submarine* (1968). There was also a string of popular movies starring Elvis Presley singing his way through various jobs and situations, the best probably being *Change of Habit* (1969), where he played a young doctor. To compete, Britain had Cliff Richard appearing in upbeat films such as *The Young Ones* (1961) and *Summer Holiday* (1962).

Westerns remained as popular in the 1960s as they had in the 1950s, and included *The Alamo* (1960), *The Sons of Katie Elder* (1965), and *Butch Cassidy and the Sundance Kid* (1969). There were many more featuring stars such as Paul Newman, Steve McQueen, Clint Eastwood, Yul Brynner and, of course, John Wayne.

Other popular films of the 1960s that appealed to children included *Swiss Family Robinson* (1960), which told the story of a family stranded on a desert island and their struggle to survive. While there, they have many adventures, including fights with pirates, before they are eventually rescued. The film starred John Mills, Dorothy McGuire and James MacArthur.

Mary Poppins (1964) was one of the most memorable films of the 1960s for children, and starred Julie Andrews as the nanny Mary Poppins, who took care of her charges, Jane and Michael Banks, while introducing them to many adventures. Dick Van Dyke played the Cockney chimney sweep who accompanied them. The film is famous for many memorable songs, including 'Jolly Holiday', 'A Spoonful of Sugar' and 'Supercalifragilisticexpialidocious', which was repeated by every child in the playground. It was probably one of Walt Disney's best films, and is fondly remembered. Other successful Walt Disney movies included *One Hundred and One Dalmatians* (1961), *The Jungle Book* (1967) and *Blackbeard's Ghost* (1968).

A Hard Day's Night (1964) came at the height of The Beatles' popularity, and was hugely successful at the time. It told the story of a day in the life of the Beatles and featured whacky, zany comedy as the band tried to get to a television studio to perform a live concert. Wilfred Brambell (*Steptoe and Son*) played Paul's grandfather, and the film also featured Victor Spinetti, Deryck Guyler, Lionel Blair and John Junkin. Besides the title track, other songs featured include 'Can't Buy Me Love', 'She Loves You', and 'This Boy'.

The Sound of Music (1965) featured some of the most recognisable songs from a musical, including 'Do-Re-Mi', 'My Favourite Things', and 'Edelweiss'. 'Do-Re-Mi' was sung in school classes up and down the land. The film starred Julie Andrews as a would-be nun who is employed as a governess to the singing children of Georg von Trapp in Austria during the 1930s. Maria (Julie Andrews) falls in love with von Trapp (Christopher Plummer) and the movie follows their story, ending with them escaping from the Nazis. The film was hugely successful and is fondly remembered.

Born Free (1966) told the true story of Joy and George Adamson as they tried to raise a lion cub, Elsa, in Kenya. The film starred real-life husband and wife, Virginia McKenna and Bill Travers, in the lead roles, and is memorable for the theme song, sung by Matt Monro.

Those Magnificent Men in Their Flying Machines (1965) featured a race from London to Paris and efforts to sabotage planes along the way. Terry-Thomas is well remembered as the Dick Dastardly-like Sir Percy Ware-Armitage. Other cast members included Stuart Whitman, Sarah Miles and James Fox. *Monte Carlo or Bust!* (1969) followed a similar story and again featured Terry-Thomas, along with major stars including Tony Curtis, Jack Hawkins and Peter Cook. It was all very similar to the popular cartoon *Wacky Races*.

Fantastic Voyage (1966) was a science fiction movie that featured adventure, espionage and miniaturisation. Stephen Boyd played a government agent, Charles Grant, who, together with Captain Bill Owens (played by William Redfield), Dr Michaels (Donald Pleasence), Dr Peter Duval (Arthur (Kennedy) and his assistant Cora Peterson (Raquel Welch), is placed on board a submarine which is then miniaturised and injected into the body of scientist Jan Benes, who lies comatose in hospital with a brain clot. The aim of the crew is to remove the clot before the sub returns to its normal size.

Bonnie and Clyde (1967) starred Faye Dunnaway and Warren Beatty, and followed their criminal escapades around America. Although based on a true story, it was somewhat glamourised. The most memorable scene is when the duo are ambushed by FBI officers and machine-gunned. Everyone seeing the film at the time expected to hear Georgie Fame's hit *The Ballard of Bonnie and Clyde* as the theme tune, but it wasn't featured. However, the song went to number one in the UK charts in 1967.

Doctor Doolittle (1967) featured Rex Harrison as a doctor who could talk to animals. Doolittle is later accused of murder when he helps a seal escape from the circus dressed in women's clothing. The seal, who wants to visit her husband at the North Pole, is seen by two fishermen as Doolittle throws her off a cliff. Doolittle escapes prison with the aid of several animals, his niece Emma Fairfax (Samantha Eggar), and Matthew Mugg (Anthony Newley). The film follows his adventures around the globe and ends with the animals of England going on strike in protest against his sentence. The film is best remembered for the Pushmi-Pullyu. The movie was an incredible hit with children and spawned much merchandise.

Oliver! (1968) was a huge success for composer Lionel Bart. The film featured Mark Lester as the orphan Oliver Twist (based on the book by Charles Dickens). The film is remembered for the famous scene where Oliver holds up his bowl at the workhouse and asks, 'Please, Sir? Can I have some more?' The film contained some very memorable songs, including 'Food, Glorious, Food', 'Consider Yourself' and 'You've Got to Pick a Pocket or Two'. Co-stars included Ron Moody (Fagin), Shani Wallis (Nancy), Oliver Reed (Bill Sikes), Harry Secombe (Bumble) and Jack Wild (the Artful Dodger).

Chitty Chitty Bang Bang (1968) was a big hit with children during 1968, and featured Dick Van Dyke as the inventor Caractacus Potts. Potts invents a flying car which a dictator from a foreign country wants to steal. Together with his two children, Jeremy and Jemima, they journey to the land of Vulgaria to fight the evil Baron Bomburst. There are many memorable tunes along the way, including 'Truly Scrumptious', 'Hushabye Mountain' and, of course, 'Chitty Chitty Bang Bang'. The film was based on a novel by James Bond's creator, Ian Fleming. The success of the film ensured huge sales of Corgi's Chitty Chitty Bang Bang car (most boys had one).

Of course, there were many other iconic and successful films of the decade that weren't appealing to children but were huge box office hits. These included *Spartacus* (1960), *Psycho* (1960), *Dr Zhivago* (1965), and *Easy Rider* (1969).

There were so many excellent films made in the 1960s that it would be impossible to name them all. The decade produced some of the most memorable movies of all time, and many proved very influential in subsequent years.

Comics in the 1960s were many and varied. Many came with free gifts, which included things like balsa aeroplanes, whistles, plastic toys and jokes. The *Beano* had been a favourite comic for boys since the 1930s. By the 1960s, it was still as popular as ever, and featured Biffo the Bear on the cover as the main strip. Other popular strips of the 1960s included the Bash Street Kids, Little Plum (the son of a Red

Indian) and Billy the Cat. The comic has been read and enjoyed by generations of children and, today, is still much loved.

The *Beezer* (1956–93) was a well-loved comic that entertained children for almost forty years. It came in A3 size (like its sister comic, *Topper*), which made it twice as big as other comics. Popular characters in the *Beezer* during the 1960s included The Hillys and the Billies, The Banana Bunch and Dicky Burd.

The Boy's Own Paper (1879–1967) was first introduced in 1879, and was published to educate and instil Christian morals into young people's minds. It contained a mixture of adventure stories, puzzles, nature study, sports and games and essay competitions. Authors who contributed to early copies included Jules Verne, Arthur Conan-Doyle and R. M. Ballantyne. By the 1960s, contributors included the astronomer Patrick Moore and science fiction writer Isaac Asimov.

Boy's World (1963–64) ran for eighty-nine issues before merging with the hugely successful *Eagle*.

Bunty (1958–2001) was aimed at girls, and featured short comic strip stories as well as a letters page, puzzles and competitions. The back page featured a cut-out doll with paper clothes. Regular strips included The Four Marys, about four teenage girls living at a boarding school; Bunty – 'a girl like you' – about a blonde girl and her friends Haya and Payal; and Princess of the Pops.

Buster (1960–2000) was a favourite comic of many. When the comic was first released in 1960, an advert in the *Daily Mirror* announced that Buster was the son of their own comic strip character, Andy Capp. The first issue, published on 23 May 1960, had an all-important free gift – a 'Balloon Bleeper!' The free gift with Issue 2 was a 'Zoomer Jet', which you whizzed around your head on a piece of string. Issue 3 gave away a 'Fool 'Em All Dodger Kit', which consisted of a false nose, moustache and glasses. The comic cost 4*d*, and popular characters included Tony Broke, Chalky, Odd Ball, Joker and Fuss Pot.

Film Fun (1920–1962) was hugely popular, and had a circulation of approximately 800,000 copies a week pre-war. It featured all the famous film stars of the day in comic form. The first issue featured Harold Lloyd on its cover. However, by 1962, sales figures had dropped dramatically, and *Film Fun* was merged with *Buster*.

Radio Fun (1938–61) contained mainly comic strips of popular radio and film stars. These included Benny Hill, Charlie Drake, and Jack Warner. It came to an end in February 1961 when it merged with *Buster*.

Commando Comics (1961–present) featured stories from the First and Second World War. The pocket-sized comic became one of the most popular British war comics. It was launched by D. C. Thomson (who also published the *Beano* and the *Dandy*) in 1961, and featured tales of loyalty, courage, cowardice and patriotism.

Comic strips featuring the Daleks appeared regularly in *TV Century 21* as well as *TV Comic* during the 1960s and later, in the 1970s, appeared in *Countdown*, *TV Action* and *Doctor Who Magazine*.

The Dandy (1937–2012) first came out in 1937. It and the *Beano* were published on alternate weeks during the Second World War because of paper and ink rationing. By 1949, normal weekly publishing had recommenced, and during the 1960s, the comic was well read by boys all over the country. Popular characters in the *Dandy* included Korky the Cat and Desperate Dan, which became the comic's longest-running strips. The first issue of the *Dandy* was published on 4 December 1937. It was then known as *The Dandy Comic*. It was different from other comics of the day because it used speech balloons instead of captions. The first *Dandy* annual was released in 1938 and was originally called *The Dandy Monster Comic*. An annual has been published every year since. The annuals always came out at Christmastime, and boys in the 1960s all loved getting a copy of the *Dandy* or the *Beano* as a Christmas present. In 1954, the first Desperate Dan Book was published. It mostly consisted of strips that had appeared in the comic throughout the year. The *Dandy* eventually consisted only of comic strips, but the earlier issues had also included text strips with few illustrations. Some of these text strips included Jimmy's Pocket Grandpa, British Boys, and Girls Go West. Sales eventually slumped from 2 million a week in the 1950s to just 8,000 a week sixty years later, leading to the comic closing in December 2012.

The Eagle (1950–69) first appeared on 14 April 1950. Within its pages were strips featuring Captain Pugwash and Dan Dare. The comic was the idea of Marcus Morris, who was an Anglican vicar from Lancashire. Previously, Morris had edited a parish church magazine called the *Anvil*, which was illustrated by Frank Hampson. Morris felt that the *Anvil* wasn't communicating the word of the Church to a large audience so with Hampson, he created a mock-up comic book featuring Christian values. The idea was offered to several Fleet Street publishers but little interest was shown in it. However, eventually the Hulton Press took on the idea and the *Eagle* was born. A huge publicity campaign ensured that the first issue sold over 900,000 copies. The front page featured, in full colour, 'Dan Dare, Pilot of the Future'. The cover was drawn by Hampson. Other characters appearing in the comic included 'Riders of the Range' and 'PC 49'. There were also news and sport sections, together with cutaway drawings of complicated machinery. Readers could join a club, which offered all sorts of merchandise for sale including toothpaste, pyjamas and toy ray guns. There were several disputes when the comic was taken over by a new publisher, and Morris left in 1959, with Hampson leaving soon after.

Lion (1952–74) was a weekly boys' adventure comic, published by Fleetway and designed to compete with the *Eagle*. Its main feature was Captain Condor – Space Ship Pilot, which was very similar to the *Eagle*'s Dan Dare. One of the comic's most popular characters was Robot Archie. It also had a letters page run by Reg 'Skipper' Clarke. Prince Charles was an avid reader when he was a boy and the comic was said to be delivered to Buckingham Palace every Friday. In 1969, it merged with the *Eagle* and later *Thunder* in 1971 before joining *Valiant* in 1974.

Swift (1954–63) was published as a junior companion to the *Eagle*. It was originally published by the Hulton Press, but when the company was sold to Odhams Press in 1959, *Swift* merged with the *Eagle*. Regular strips included Smiley (which featured on the front cover), Ginger and Co., and Sir Boldasbrass.

Tiger (1954–85) was originally launched in 1954 under the title '*Tiger – The Sport and Adventure Picture Story Weekly*'. Its most popular strip was Roy of the Rovers, which told the story of fictional footballer Roy Race and his team, Melchester Rovers. The strip became so popular that eventually Roy of the Rovers had his own comic. *Tiger* merged with several comics over the following years, becoming *Tiger and Hurricane*, *Tiger and Jag*, and *Tiger and Scorcher*, before finally merging with the *Eagle*.

Girl (1951–64) was a comic aimed solely at girls. There were many comics for boys, particularly the *Eagle*, on the market and it was felt that a similar comic should be produced for girls. The first copy appeared on 2 November 1951 and featured 'Kitty Hawke and her All-Girl Air Crew'. The comic was a sister paper to the *Eagle* and was again produced by the Hulton Press, with most of its pages in full colour. The idea was again that of the Reverend Marcus Morris and the main story was illustrated by Ray Bailey. The Kitty Hawke strip proved not to be very popular and was thought to be too masculine. It featured the exploits of a group of women who ran a chartered airline. Perhaps it was too much like the Dan Dare strip on the cover of the *Eagle*. Eventually, the strip was moved inside the comic to its black-and-white pages, and 'Wendy and Jinx' was moved to the front cover. Wendy and Jinx told the story of two girls at Manor School and stayed on the cover until 1958. Other stories within the comic included Angela Air Hostess, At Work with Janet – Fashion Artist, Belle of the Ballet, Emergency Ward 10 (based on the popular television series), Lindy Love and Susan of St Brides. The first issue cost 4½d. The comic continued throughout the 1950s and was eventually merged with *Princess* in 1964.

The Hornet (1963–76) ran for 648 issues before merging with the *Hotspur* in 1976. The first issue came with a free gift, which was a balsa wood Kestrel Glider. Popular strips featured in the comic included The Blazing Ace of Space and V for Vengeance.

The *Hotspur* (1933–81) was originally a story paper for boys but it was relaunched as a comic in 1959 and was renamed the *New Hotspur*. Popular strips included Coral Island, Jonny Jett, King Cobra, Spring-Heeled Jack, Union Jack Jackson and X-Bow. It was eventually incorporated into *The Victor* in 1981.

Jack and Jill (1954–85) regularly featured Jack and Jill of Buttercup Farm on the front page, and was based on the well-loved nursery rhyme. The stories were told in rhyming couplets and regular characters within the comic included Harold Hare, Teddy and Cuddly, Flipper the Skipper, Chalky the Blackboard Boy and Douglas Dachshund.

Jackie (1964–93) was a favourite girls' magazine for many years, especially in the 1960s and 1970s. It was the bestselling teen magazine in the UK for ten years and included pop pin-ups, fashion and beauty tips, gossip, comic strips and short stories.

Knockout (1939–63) was launched by the Amalgamated Press (later Fleetway Publications) in direct competition with the *Beano* and the *Dandy*. It featured a mixture of comic strips and adventure stories. It absorbed the *Magnet* in 1940 and *Comic Cuts* in 1953 before merging with *Valiant* in 1963. Popular strips included Kelly's Eye, Battler Britton, Davy Crockett and Hopalong Cassidy.

Look and Learn (1962–82) was popular with teachers and parents because, although it was a comic, it was also educational. Piles of the comics could be found in classrooms of the 1960s and were read when it was too wet to play out during break times. It contained a variety of interesting articles featuring information on topics from volcanoes to the Loch Ness monster. There was also a long-running science fiction strip called The Trigan Empire. Its worldwide pen pal pages proved very popular. The first issue sold 700,000 copies, but this settled down to about 300,000 for later issues. Early features included stories about Charles I, Vincent Van Gogh, The Arabian Nights and Three Men in a Boat.

Mandy (1967–91) was a British comic for girls that was first issued in January 1967. The first issue featured a free Rainbow Ring. Popular strips included Glenda the Guide, Skeleton Corner, Very Important Pupil and The Girls at Knock-Out Academy. Most stories were serialised and lasted for between eight and twelve issues.

Pippin (1966–86) was published by Polystyle Publications and featured characters from preschool television shows. Regular strips included The Pogles, Andy Pandy, and Chigley as well as many others. The comic also featured a puzzle page, readers' letters and a story from the Bible.

Playhour (1954–87) was a companion comic to Jack and Jill but aimed at slightly older children. The comic contained tales of television favourites such as Pinky and Perky, Bill and Ben and Sooty. Other stories included Billy Brock's Schooldays, The Wonderful Tales of Willow Wood, and Norman Gnome.

Pow! (1967–68) first appeared in January 1967, and the following year it merged with its sister comic, *Wham!* This followed a merger with Power Comics' other popular title, *Smash!* Power Comics was an imprint of IPC's Odham Press division and published reprints from American Marvel comics featuring superheroes including Spiderman and the Fantastic Four. The comic also featured Nick Fury Agent of Shield, which was drawn by Jack Kirby. Most of the comic contained humour strips, such as The Dolls of St Dominics, Wee Willie Haggis and The Spy from Skye. Adventure scripts included The Python and Jack Magic.

Robin (1953–69) was published by Hulton Press and was a companion comic to *Eagle*, *Girl* and *Swift* but was aimed at a younger readership. Regular strips included Andy Pandy, Flower Pot Men, and The Story of Woppit.

Smash! (1966–71) ran for 257 issues from February 1966 until it merged with *Valiant* in 1971. Marvel comic strips were first introduced into the comic in Issue 16, with reprints of stories about the Incredible Hulk. Other Marvel stories appeared later, including the adventures of the Fantastic Four, The Avengers and Daredevil. DC Comics' strip Batman appeared from Issue 20, after the television show starring Adam West became immensely popular. There were also humorous comic strips featured, including The Man from B.U.N.G.L.E., Charlie's Choice, and The Nervs.

Terrific (1967–68) was another comic issued by Odhams Press under the Power Comics imprint. It ran for forty-three issues before merging with *Fantastic*. Again, it featured reprints of Marvel superhero strips, and Thor was often featured on its cover. Other Marvel strips featured in *Terrific* included Sub-Mariner and Giant-man from the comic *Tales to Astonish*.

Fantastic (1967–68) first appeared in February 1967 and merged with *Terrific* in 1968, going on to feature more Marvel superheroes including Thor, the Avengers and Doctor Strange.

The most popular strip in the *Topper* (1953–90) was Mickey the Monkey, who appeared on the front page of the comic for many years. He was very similar to Biffo the Bear in the *Beano*. Other well-loved characters included Beryl the Peril, Desert Island Dick, and Sir Laughalot. In 1990, the comic was merged with another long-running D. C. Thomson title, the *Beezer*. *Sparky* (1965–77) was published weekly by D. C. Thomson and ran from January 1965 until July 1977 when it was merged with another popular comic, the *Topper*. Originally, it was aimed at a slightly younger audience than the *Beano* and the *Dandy*. Popular characters included Sparky, Dreamy Dave and Dozy Dora, and Keyhole Kate.

In 1965, with the success of Gerry Anderson's show *Stingray* on television, the series was given its own comic, *TV Century 21* (1965–71). Over the years, the comic featured strips from Fireball XL5, Thunderbirds, and Joe 90. Other non-Gerry Anderson strips included Star Trek and Land of the Giants. The Daleks also made regular appearances. In 1968, the comic merged with *TV Tornado*.

All British comics produced their own annuals, which were a must for Christmas presents and were eagerly looked forward to. They featured collections of strips from well-loved comics as well as the latest television characters and cartoons.

Most children would receive several annuals for Christmas and these often included the *Beano* and the *Dandy*, which were favourites for many years.

American comics featured glossier covers and full-colour strips. Adverts within their pages featured X-ray Specs, Sea Monkeys and Charles Atlas's bodybuilding course. X-ray specs apparently allowed you to see through your hand and people's clothing. They were made of cardboard with two eyeholes cut out which contained feathers. Looking through the feathers gave the illusion of being able to see through things. The advert for Sea Monkeys showed a family of creatures in a fishbowl smiling and doing tricks. Even in the advert, they looked nothing like monkeys (more like aliens) and there was more disappointment to come. Once the kit arrived (a sealed packet of powder), the 'monkeys' turned out to be nothing more than tiny shrimps when added to water. Charles Atlas's bodybuilding course featured an advert showing a thin teenager, at the beach, having sand kicked in his face by other youths. After taking the bodybuilding course, he was able to sort out the bullies and soon had a wonderful girlfriend. Other adverts included writing and art courses as well as many other strange and peculiar products that only could be found in American comics.

Some of the best American comic books included *Batman*, *Casper the Friendly Ghost*, and *Superman*. There was something weird and wonderful, at the time, about anything that came from America, and their comics and sense of humour differed greatly from the humour that was found in British comics such as the *Beano* and the *Dandy*.

Comics were well read and much loved by children during the 1960s and many are still very fondly remembered today.

Children learned to read at school by using Janet and John books, as well as a huge range of titles published by Ladybird. Originally Janet and John books had been published in America, but in 1949, publishers James Nisbet & Co. licensed the books to Great Britain and they became immensely popular for early school readers in the 1950s and 1960s. The books featured English children living a middle-class life. The books were illustrated by Florence and Margaret Hoopes. By the 1970s, the books had become outdated and were less popular as teaching aids.

Ladybird books first appeared in 1915 and were published by Wills & Hepworth. All carried the distinct Ladybird logo. In 1964, the company started producing their Key Words Reading Scheme series, which was used extensively in schools all over Great Britain. The series contained thirty-six small-format hardback books. In the 1960s, the Learnabout series was published. Ladybird books covered a whole range of subjects including fairy tales, fiction, science, history, geography, wildlife, sport, transport, royalty and classic tales.

Enid Blyton's books have been read by generations and sum up many people's childhoods. Her popular books included adventures featuring Noddy and the Three Golliwogs but the most fondly remembered featured the Famous Five and the Secret Seven. The first Famous Five book, *Five on a Treasure Island*, was published in 1942. It featured a group of young children who were Julian, Dick, Anne and Georgina, who was more commonly known as George. They were accompanied on their adventures by Timmy the dog. All the stories took place in the summer holidays when the children met up after returning from their respective boarding schools. Enid Blyton wrote twenty-one books featuring the Famous Five, the last one being *Five Are Together Again*, which was published in 1963. The books were hugely successful and sold millions, as did the books in her similar series, The Secret Seven. The Secret Seven included Peter, Janet (Peter's sister), Jack, Barbara, George, Pam and Colin. Another well-read series of Enid Blyton books was the Five Find-Outers. Characters featured included Fatty (Frederick Algernon Trotteville), who was the leader of the group, Laurence 'Larry' Daykin, Margaret 'Daisy' Daykin, Philip 'Pip' Hilton and Elizabeth 'Bets' Hilton. They were joined by Fatty's Scottish terrier, Buster. The series of mystery books was published between 1943 and 1969 and included fifteen different stories including *The Mystery of the Burnt Cottage*, *The Mystery of the Disappearing Cat* and *The Mystery of the Secret Room*.

Popular fiction for children during the 1960s included *The Lion, the Witch and the Wardrobe*, which was published in 1950 and written by C. S. Lewis. Geoffrey Bles, who published the book, feared that tales of fantasy might not be well received, but children loved the book and soon after several other works in the Narnia saga were published including *Prince Caspian: The Return to Narnia* (1951), *The Voyage of the Dawn Treader* (1952), *The Silver Chair* (1953), *The Horse and His Boy* (1954), *The Magician's Nephew* (1955) and *The Last Battle* (1956).

Books featuring the character Biggles, by Captain W. E. Johns, were widely read in the 1960s. Captain W. E. Johns was the pen name of William Earl Johns. He had never actually held the rank of captain but was himself a pilot during the First World War and was captured in September 1918. He remained a prisoner until the end of the war. He wrote over 160 books, nearly 100 of them featuring Biggles.

The character of Biggles was said to be based on Air Commander Cecil George Wigglesworth, whom Johns had known during the First World War. Johns continued to write books about Biggles until his death in 1968.

Warne's Observer books were published between 1937 and 2003, and were very popular with children. The small hardback books could fit in your pocket and featured subjects including birds, aircraft, and dogs. They were ideal for any inquisitive mind and, in a time when children played outside more, they were a great way of discovering information about the world around.

I-Spy books were equally popular. An article in the *News Chronicle* every day featured 'Big Chief I-Spy' (the head of the Redskins) and recorded his I-Spy triumphs in tracking and spotting. Messages and passwords were printed for members of the I-Spy club, who were known as the Great Tribe. Booklets could be bought for 6*d* and covered subjects such as I-Spy insects, the unusual, and on the road. The books contained many illustrations, and the I-Spyer had to spot the objects and write down when and where the item was spotted. For each one seen, points were awarded. When the book was full, it could be sent to Big Chief I-Spy and an Order of Merit would be returned, together with the booklet. The books had to be signed by a teacher or parents along with the name of the entrant's school. The craze proved incredibly popular and it continues today although perhaps it's not quite the same. Charles Warrell produced the first I-Spy booklet in 1948, and by 1956, Arnold Cawthrow had become the second Big Chief I-Spy.

Books featuring Rupert Bear were also immensely popular in the 1960s. Rupert had first appeared in the *Daily Express* on 8 November 1920 to boost sales and to compete with their rivals, the *Daily Mail* and the *Daily Mirror*. By 1935, the stories were being told and illustrated by Arthur Bestall who had previously illustrated *Punch*. He continued to illustrate the Rupert comic strips until he was well into his nineties. From 1936, a Rupert annual was published, and thousands of children were given them for Christmas presents. Some of the annuals of the 1960s contained 'Magic Paintings', which allowed the reader to take a paintbrush over a picture using just water and they would be magically coloured in. They are fondly remembered and much sought after today by collectors. In 1969, Rupert appeared in his first television series, *The Adventures of Rupert Bear*.

Classic stories such as *Treasure Island*, *Robinson Crusoe*, *The Swiss Family Robinson*, Robin Hood and William Tell continued in popularity throughout the 1960s, although they had been around for many years. All featured adventurous tales which appealed to any young boy who enjoyed emulating pirates, outlaws or other exciting characters while playing outdoors.

Treasure Island was first published in 1883 and was written by Scottish author Robert Louis Stevenson. It was a story of pirates and buried treasure and had originally been serialised in the children's magazine *Young Folks* between 1881 and 1882. It famously featured Long John Silver in a story narrated by Jim Hawkins. In the 1960s, every boy could recite the song sung by Billy Bones in the book – 'Fifteen men on the dead man's chest, Yo-ho-ho, and a bottle of rum!' The book was adapted for both film and television many times. In 1968, the BBC made nine twenty-five-minute episodes of *Treasure Island*, which featured Peter Vaughan, later famous for playing Grouty in *Porridge*.

Robinson Crusoe was another very popular book with boys. A thirteen-part serial, *The Adventures of Robinson Crusoe*, was first aired on the BBC in 1965 and was repeated often. The television show was originally made in France and dubbed into English. At the same time, its memorable musical soundtrack was added. The original book was written by Daniel Defoe and was first published in 1719. It told the tale of a castaway stranded on a desert island near Trinidad. While there, he encountered cannibals and mutineers before being finally rescued. The book was thought to be based on the story of Alexander Selkirk, a Scottish castaway who had been stranded on an island in the Pacific called Más a Tierra. The island was renamed *Robinson Crusoe Island* in 1966. The book hasn't lost any of its charm over the several hundred years since it was first written, and, together with the television series, fuelled the imaginations of children in the 1960s.

Gulliver's Travels was a novel originally published in 1726 and was written by an Irish author and clergyman, Jonathan Swift. At the time, it was universally read, and it has remained in print ever since. During the 1960s, two television shows were made based on the book. The first, *The Three Worlds of Gulliver*, was first broadcast in 1960. It starred Kerwin Mathews and featured special effects by Ray Harryhausen. In 1968, Hanna-Barbera produced a cartoon called *The Adventures of Gulliver*. The book tells of Lemuel Gulliver's voyages around the globe. In his first adventure, he finds himself washed ashore after a shipwreck and becomes the prisoner of little people on the island of Lilliput. The same idea was also later used in the successful television show *Land of the Giants*. At first, Gulliver is seen as an enemy of the Lilliputians but later becomes their hero before displeasing the king and his court. He makes his escape and his second adventure takes him to the land of Brobdingnag, which is inhabited by giants. There are many more voyages and adventures featured in the book, although his visit to Lilliput is the most retold and well-known story.

Every boy wanted to be Robin Hood in the early 1960s especially with the success of the television show *The Adventures of Robin Hood*, starring Richard Greene. The show was made in the 1950s but continued to be shown throughout the 1960s. Every boy who had ever climbed a tree or played in the woods imagined himself as Robin Hood. There were many books written about the outlaw, but *The Merry Adventures of Robin Hood*, written by Howard Pyle in 1883, has been the most enduring over the generations. The book follows Hood as he first becomes an outlaw and tells the tales of the Merry Men, which included Little John, Friar Tuck and Allan-a-Dale.

The Swiss Family Robinson was an all-action adventure story about a family shipwrecked in the East Indies while en route to Port Jackson in Australia. The book was first published in 1812 and was written by Johann David Wyss, a Swiss pastor. The story featured the family's struggle to survive on a desert island and their numerous adventures before finally being rescued. In 1960, Walt Disney made a film of the book, which was hugely successful, starring John Mills. The 1960s television series *Lost in Space* was loosely based on the book and featured the story of a futuristic family, also called Robinson, who found themselves stranded in space.

The Bible was also well read by children in the 1960s. All schools had religious teachings at the time and many children were given bibles by their schools to read and learn. To many, the stories were just as interesting and exciting as stories by Enid Blyton, especially when read outloud by a teacher in class.

There were many other wonderful books read throughout the 1960s. Most featured adventures that appealed to the imaginations of young children, many of whom spent most of their leisure time, when not reading, outdoors.

1. A family at the fair in the early 1960s. Those are real monkeys! Popular rides included the dodgems, the helter-skelter, the waltzer and the carousel. Slot machines, hoopla and shoot-'em-up games were always well liked also.

2. The family car. One of the most popular cars of the 1960s was the Ford Prefect. This model, a 107E, was made up until 1961, but the cars were seen for many years afterwards. Ford replaced the model with the Consul Classic.

3. Boys loved playing cowboys and Indians, and dressing up as one or the other was a lot of fun. Every boy had his own bow and arrow, usually with stoppers on the end of the arrows to prevent injuries.

4. Lego and an ice lolly on a hot summer's day. Everyone loved playing with Lego, which has been well loved since the late 1950s, when the modern Lego brick was patented. Building a train, boat or car was popular with all boys in the 1960s. Lego has since advanced greatly.

Above: 5. Fun at the seaside. A trip to the seaside was an adventure, and every family had a lilo for the kids. Inflatable water wings were also handy for children who couldn't swim, and every boy and girl had their own bucket and spade to build sandcastles.

Left: 6. The local park. Most parks in the 1960s featured some sort of concrete vehicle, usually a car, train or ship. Most parks had a slide, a roundabout and swings. Floors were made from hard concrete so there were always some banged heads or grazed knees.

7. Feeding the swans was an exciting pastime for a small boy, as shown in this photo.

8. Fun in the sea. All children had a great time on a day trip to the seaside, even the ones who couldn't swim.

9. A boy and his tin robot. Tin robots from Japan talked, walked and fired guns. Japanese toys were very advanced for the time and had clever internal workings. Japan made other tin toys such as police cars, aeroplanes and spaceships.

10. Fun at the park in the late 1960s. This photograph shows the variety of playing apparatus that appeared in parks at the time. This one has a hobby horse, a metal climbing frame and even a full-size steam roller.

11. Spacehoppers became the must-have toy in 1969, and this continued well into the 1970s. Much fun was to be had bouncing around the garden or in the front room. For a few years, spacehoppers became a major craze.

12. A Horikawa Japanese tin robot. This robot did many things, including walking, spinning around, flashing lights and firing guns.

13. A selection of LPs and singles from the 1960s. Shown here is The Rolling Stones' first album, 'Yellow Submarine' by The Beatles, 'Sounds of Silence' by Simon and Garfunkel, 'Revolver' by The Beatles and 'Pisces, Aquarius, Capricorn & Jones Ltd' by The Monkees. The single shown is 'Return to Sender' by Elvis Presley.

14. A Bank of England £1 note. Pound notes were equivalent to 20s and certainly went a lot further in the 1960s. The pound remained in note form until 1983, when the pound coin was introduced.

Left: 15. An advert for Action Transfers, 1969. Action Transfers, made by Letraset, were very popular with boys. The transfers could be rubbed onto card backgrounds using a coin or a pencil. Popular Action Transfers included footballers, spacemen and historical events. A set featuring Tarzan was given away with the breakfast cereals Shredded Wheat and Cubs.

Below: 16. An Airfix motor racing set complete with track and controllers. Similar to Scalextric, the Airfix kit allowed its owners to race cars around a track using electronic handsets connected to a transformer. The set shown here featured two Mini Coopers.

17. Buzz Aldrin was the second man on the moon in July 1969 as part of the Apollo 11 mission. Many of the iconic astronaut shots feature Buzz Aldrin, as several were taken by Neil Armstrong.

18. Wade Whimsie dinosaur characters. These were given away as free gifts with Flintstones Christmas crackers in 1965.

19. Historical vehicles given away inside Kellogg's cereal in the 1960s. Most cereals gave away a free toy inside their packets and they were sought after at the time. They included plastic figures, vehicles and many other items.

20. Buzz Aldrin on the moon's surface in July 1969. This iconic photo was taken by Neil Armstrong using a specially adapted Hasselblad camera.

21. The *Apollo 11* team, including Neil Armstrong, Michael Collins and Buzz Aldrin. While Neil Armstrong and Buzz Aldrin walked on the moon, Michael Collins remained in the lunar module.

Above: 22. A Corgi Batmobile. With the popularity of the television series starring Adam West and Burt Ward, the Batmobile became a sought-after toy, and most boys had one. It came complete with detachable Batman and Robin plastic figures, rockets and a launcher, and a chain cutter at the front.

Left: 23. An Airfix Motor Ace set. The set gave you all the excitement of a proper motor race and included racing cars, tracks and transformer, all for £13 15s. Other sets included racing Minis as well as various other makes of car, such as Ferrari, Mercedes and Lotus.

24. An advert for Corgi Majors from 1965. This one features a Ford tilt car with detachable trailer. Other vehicles shown in the advert include an American Chevrolet police car, Chipperfield's Circus publicity van, a Chevrolet Impala and a Chrysler Imperial, complete with opening doors, boot and bonnet.

25. Christmas Airfix gifts, 1967. Every boy loved Airfix kits, which included cars, ships and historical figures, for Christmas. Also shown in the advert is the Airfix art set, with painting by numbers, and the Monte Carlo racing set.

26. Corgi's Batmobile – a must-have for every boy, and probably one of Corgi's most popular toys ever. Other popular television vehicles featured on the advert included the Saint's Volvo, the Thrushbuster from the *Man from U.N.C.L.E.*, The Avengers' Bentley and Lotus, and James Bond's Aston Martin DB5.

27. Corgi's Rockets. Rocket tracks were the must-have toy at the end of the 1960s. The track was made from red plastic that could form loop-de-loops, ramps and sharp bends. Some tracks would spread all around a boy's bedroom, and the various cars that could be bought, called Rocket Racers, were made to perform all kinds of tricks.

PREFECT

28. A school prefect's badge. Any kid who was respected in class could find themselves a prefect. Duties involved looking out for other kids and making sure that everyone behaved themselves, especially in assembly and in the playground. Stopping boys running in corridors was another duty.

29. An Airfix competition featured in comics during 1969. This competition offered exciting prizes, including all the latest Airfix models.

30. Corgi toys for 1964. All the latest models can be seen in this advert, including a London taxi, complete with policeman, a double-decker bus and a Commer milk float.

31. Corgi toys for 1965. The 1965 advert featured a Ford Mustang and a Lotus Elan as well as a tractor and hydraulic tower wagon. The tractor cost 11s 9d, and was ideal for any farm set.

Above: 32. A Dansette radio, at the time, was the latest portable radio, and could be carried easily around the house or, perhaps, taken to a friend's.

Left: 33. An Alps Japanese tin robot. This robot was very popular with boys and took two large batteries, which enabled it to walk while showing a space scene in its television chest.

Left: 34. An advert for Corgi Racing Cars, featuring the Formula 1 Cooper Maserati, the MGC GT, the Ghia 5000 Mangusta, the Jaguar E Type and Ferrari Berlinetta 250 le Mans.

Below: 35. An advert for Standard Fireworks. On 5 November, every dad would make sure he had a box of fireworks for the kids, and these would be let off in the garden. Popular ones included Catherine wheels, Roman candles and rockets, which were fired from a milk bottle.

Left: 36. Corgi Toys Are Go! This advert from 1967 features the popular Daktari jeep complete with all the characters from the television show, including Dr Marsh Tracy, Paula, Judy the Chimp and Clarence the cross-eyed lion. The jeep was later given away as part of a Tarzan promotion on cereal.

Below: 37. Three of Corgi's bestselling cars in the 1960s, including the Batmobile, the Thrushbuster from the *Man from U.N.C.L.E* and James Bond's Aston Martin DB5 from *Goldfinger.*

Left: 38. A Horikawa Japanese tin robot which walked and fired guns from its chest before spinning around. Robots were featured in many television series, especially ones from Japan.

Below: 39. Conkers and marbles, simple toys that kept boys occupied for hours in the playground during the spring, summer and autumn. Both were much prized, and there was lots of fun finding the best conker tree.

Above: 40. A Japanese tin toy train. As well as robots, cars, boats and planes were also made from tin. This train featured all the noises that a steam train would make, as well as producing smoke.

Left: 41. Muhammad Ali famously beat the reigning heavyweight champion, Sonny Liston, on 25 February 1964. Before the fight he said, 'After I beat him I'm going to donate him to the zoo.'

42. A tin yo-yo featuring a spaceman. Yo-yos were very popular for many years, and new crazes for them kept reappearing. Tricks with yo-yos included 'walking the dog', 'flying saucer' and 'loop the loop'.

43. A Corgi *Man from U.N.C.L.E.* Thrushbuster, a sought-after car from the popular television series starring Robert Vaughn and David McCallum.

44. Children enjoying themselves at Butlin's. A week at the holiday camp would be talked about by children for months afterwards. Popular events for kids included the dodgems, roller skating and go-karting.

45. Children at Butlin's. While parents were out, children would be cared for by the redcoats, who put on entertainment including magic shows and comedy. Children could join the Beaver Club, and they received a badge and a certificate.

46. A Corgi Chitty Chitty Bang Bang car; was one of Corgi's most popular cars in the 1960s due to the success of the movie starring Dick van Dyke.

47. John F. Kennedy was the 35th president of the United States from January 1961 until he was assassinated in November 1963. He was succeeded by Lyndon B. Johnson.

48. A collection of Brooke Bond cards. Children loved collecting tea cards, which featured information on wildlife, space travel, fashion, flags and trees.

49. Neil Armstrong was the first man to set foot on the moon, in July 1969, and will always be remembered for his famous quote: 'That's one small step for man, one giant leap for mankind.'

50. Corgi's James Bond DB5 car. With the popularity of James Bond and *Goldfinger* in the 1960s, the Aston Martin DB5 became Corgi's bestseller ever.

51. The Beatles became one of the most popular groups of all time, and are considered the most influential band of the rock era. The first hit, 'Love Me Do', made it into the charts in 1962. In subsequent years, they sold millions of records, and their songs were recorded by most major artists.

52. A telephone. Most families didn't have a telephone in the 1960s and would have to travel to the nearest phone box to make a call. Phones first began appearing in many homes in the early 1970s.

53. Robertson's Golliwogs. By collecting tokens from Robertson's jam jars, children could send for a golliwog badge or statuette.

54. An advert for Corgi toys featuring the *Man from U.N.C.L.E.*'s Thrushbuster. Also featured is the Corgi gift set 37, featuring racing cars from the Lotus team.

55. Jan Leeming and Gus Honeybun. Many regional stations had their own entertainment for children. Westward Television, serving the South West, had Gus Honeybun, seen here with Jan Leeming. Gus performed tricks while his co-presenter read out children's birthdays.

56. A school photograph from 1969. It shows the sorts of clothes that children wore to school in the late 1960s.

57. John F. Kennedy shown in Dallas on the day he was assassinated. Also seen in the photo is his wife, Jacqueline. Both became iconic figures of the 1960s.

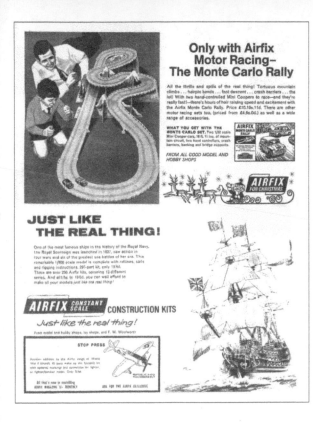

Only with Airfix Motor Racing– The Monte Carlo Rally

All the thrills and spills of the real thing! Tortuous mountain climbs . . . hairpin bends . . . fast descent . . . crash barriers . . . the lot! With two hand-controlled Mini Coopers to race—and they're really fast!—there's hours of hair raising speed and excitement with the Airfix Monte Carlo Rally. Price £10.19s.11d. There are other motor racing sets too, (priced from £4.6s.0d.) as well as a wide range of accessories.

WHAT YOU GET WITH THE MONTE CARLO SET. Two 1/32 scale Mini Cooper cars, 18 ft. 11 ins. of mountain circuit, two hand controllers, crash barriers, banking and bridge supports.

FROM ALL GOOD MODEL AND HOBBY SHOPS

AIRFIX FOR CHRISTMAS

JUST LIKE THE REAL THING!

One of the most famous ships in the history of the Royal Navy, the Royal Sovereign was launched in 1637, now action in four wars and all of the greatest sea battles of her era. This remarkably 1/600 scale model is complete with ratlines, sails and rigging instructions. 297-part kit, only 19/6d. There are over 250 Airfix kits, covering 13 different series. And all this in 1960, you can well afford to make all your models *just like the real thing!*

AIRFIX CONSTANT SCALE CONSTRUCTION KITS

Just like the real thing!

From model and hobby shops, toy shops, and F. W. Woolworth

STOP PRESS

Another addition to the Airfix range of World War II aircraft kits soon make up the Spitfire in with optional markings and connector for lighter or fighter/bomber roles. Only 3/6d.

All that's new is something
AIRFIX MAGAZINE 5/- MONTHLY   ASK FOR THE AIRFIX CATALOGUE

58. Airfix Monte Carlo rally, 1967. The racing kit was described as 'just like the real thing' and came complete with two Mini Cooper racing cars and 18 feet 11 inches of track.

59. A selection of annuals from the 1960s. Children loved getting annuals at Christmas as they featured all the characters from their favourite comics and television series.

60. A double-decker bus. Buses in the 1960s were all double-deckers and all had a conductor who would come around and collect your fare. Any misbehaving meant that you could be thrown off.

61. A selection of badges. Children loved collecting badges in the 1960s, and they came free with everything, including sweets, ice cream and lollies.

62. I-Spy booklets. Most children enjoyed I-Spy books, which featured the world around them and required them to get out and spot as much as possible. When completed, the books could be sent away, and a certificate from 'Big Chief I-Spy' would be sent back.

Above: 63. Currency of the day. Coins of the 1960s included the farthing, halfpenny, penny, threepence, sixpence, shilling, two shillings and half a crown. Several were withdrawn during the decade.

Left: 64. An advert about the withdrawal of the half crown in 1969. The coins were withdrawn in preparation for the changeover to decimal currency in 1971.

65. A visit to the zoo. Most towns had their own zoo, and children would love visiting them. Some didn't care for their animals too well, and many have disappeared over the years.

66. A dalek. Daleks were very popular during the 1960s and would scare young children whenever they appeared on *Dr Who*. Many had nightmares for weeks after!

67. Elvis Presley signing autographs. Elvis's music and films were very popular during the decade, making him one of the world's biggest stars.

68. A selection of cards given away free with ice lollies. Wall's and Lyons Maid ice cream both gave away collectable cards which could be stuck in albums or on wallcharts. These included cards from *Doctor Who*, famous people and space travel.

69. A selection of bubblegum cards. All kids liked collecting and swapping bubblegum cards, and the ones shown here are from Superman, Captain Scarlet and *The Champions*.

70. The chimes of the ice cream van had all children searching for loose change, and a queue would quickly form. Lollies were particularly popular especially the ones with connections to *Thunderbirds* and space travel. Lyons Maid and Wall's were the most popular brands.

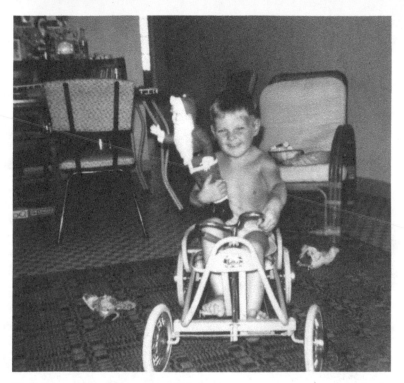

71. A boy and his go-kart in a 1960s home.

72. A 1960s family home, complete with children and Yogi Bear!

73. With more people having cars, many families made trips to the country and seaside.

74. A picture of the many models of cars driven in the 1960s.

75. A town scene from the 1960s including many cars, delivery vans and double-decker buses.

76. A town scene in the early 1960s, showing cars and the fashions of the day.

77. Before modern supermarkets, most people would buy their groceries from the local shop. The one shown here has everything needed for a household, including sweets for the children. Many shops kept the goods behind the counter, and the shopkeeper would fetch whatever was wanted.

5

School

A school day in the 1960s began at 9 a.m. Most children walked to school if it was close, or caught a bus if it was further away. It was unheard of, at the time, for parents to drive their children to school.

The day started in the playground with either a whistle being blown or a bell rung to get everyone into class. Most schools would make their pupils form an orderly straight line before they were led off into their classes, and there would be no talking.

The first event of the day would be the morning assembly, which would be presided over by the headmaster. Prayers were said before a hymn was sung, quite often 'All Things Bright and Beautiful', and the headmaster would then discuss the school events and deal with any problems such as children misbehaving or being late. Teachers in the 1960s could be quite strict, with the cane being given to anyone (usually a boy) who stepped out of line. It could also be given to children for talking in assembly or in class, or for running in the corridor, although 'lines' were often given for lesser misdemeanours. Lines involved writing the same thing, usually something like 'I shall not talk in class', 100 times. All teachers were referred to as 'Sir' or 'Miss' and there was no backchat; there'd be trouble if there was any misbehaving.

Policemen on the beat were far more common, and occasionally one would turn up in assembly. This would worry all kids who had been up to something naughty while playing outside. Sometimes, the policeman would be there to report that children had been seen playing on roofs or building sites or just getting up to general mischief. The crimes were hardly ever serious. On many occasions, a policeman would come to the school to award prizes to children who had been seen carrying out proper road safety while crossing the road.

The morning assembly usually lasted for half an hour before pupils were led to their classes. Pupils would normally be called by their surnames both when the register was called and in the classroom, and pupils would have to reply with 'Yes, sir!' or 'Yes, miss!' Heaven help any pupil who said 'yeah' instead of 'yes'.

Most children had one teacher who covered all subjects, which were usually, in junior school, maths, English, history and geography. There would also be some artwork involved and a regular fitness regime with the PE teacher. Maths included learning multiplication tables (which would be tested in class), fractions, binary numbers, long division logarithms and algebra. Most classrooms would have a wooden abacus for adding up. English involved handwriting, reading and sentence structure, and sometimes listening to the programmes for schools made specially by the BBC. At the beginning of the 1960s, this meant gathering around a radio in the classroom but later on, most schools had their own television set, although these were only black-and-white models. Colour televisions wouldn't take off until the early 1970s. History often covered the history of the British monarchy, and geography mainly mentioned lands that had once belonged to the Empire.

When the moon landings took place in July 1969, many pupils were lucky enough to see the event repeated the next day on the school television. Space travel held a great fascination for pupils at the time.

PE meant changing into a PE kit, which included white T-shirt, shorts and black gym shoes. Activities included climbing ropes, walking on parallel bars, vaulting the horse (a huge wooden contraption) and catching a medicine ball that was so heavy it could easily knock any child off his feet. PE teachers were often disciplined men, sometimes ex-Army. Games involved playing football, rounders and cricket and taking part in the annual sports day. Some schools even had their own swimming pools, but they would be unheated and covered in ice during the winter. A length of the pool was 12 yards and a double length was classed as 25 yards. Anyone who completed the distance would be awarded a certificate, which would usually be given out by the headmaster in the next assembly.

Every morning in class, the milk would be delivered and each child got a bottle of milk which measured a third of a pint. A member of the class would be allotted to hand out the milk and was known as the 'milk monitor'.

Religion played a large part in school life. As well as the morning hymns and prayers, there would also be bible stories, especially at Easter and Christmas. Christmas would also include the school nativity play, which told the story of the three wise men and the birth of Jesus.

New exercise books would be handed out to every pupil so that they could complete their work in them. These would be expected to be covered with brown paper or similar (wallpaper was popular) and there would be trouble if an exercise book was found to be uncovered. The reason was never very clear. Any other books issued, such as reading books or books on one of the subjects taken, such as maths, chemistry or physics, were also expected to be covered. Some books were quite heavy and, especially in secondary school, had to be carried home and brought in whenever they were needed. There were no lockable lockers at the time.

All pupils sat at a wooden desk facing forwards. The wooden lid, which was usually covered in the carved names of former pupils, lifted up, and inside were stored all the books needed for the day, as well as hidden items such as marbles and paper aeroplanes, etc. This was fine in junior school when children had one classroom and one teacher, but when they later went to secondary school, all books and other items had to be carted from one room to another. Younger kids had satchels for their pencils, exercise books and snacks while the older kids had leather briefcases. Some had locks but one key seemed to fit all.

At the corner of the wooden desk was a hole for an inkwell but this came from another age. By the 1960s, children at junior school were expected to use pencils while older children at secondary school could use fountain pens. Quills and pots of ink were now obsolete. Biros had been invented but weren't allowed to be used, so most kids returned home after a day writing with a leaky ink pen (they all leaked) covered in ink all over their hands.

School uniforms were worn at many schools and these usually consisted of grey flannel shorts, or a skirt for girls, shirt, tie and a home-knitted jumper for boys. Long socks were worn by both, and the phrase 'pull your socks up' was heard often from teachers to boys.

Some older boys would be made prefects, and their duties would be to look after (or tell off) younger children, stopping them from talking in assembly and running in the corridor. Some schools had a book in which the children's misdemeanours would be recorded and then read out in assembly by the headmaster. This could lead to lines, detention or, sometimes, the cane. The cane was often given for the silliest offences.

In the morning, there would be a break when all the children would run out into the playground to play games like 'it' (or 'tag') or, for girls, hopscotch or skipping. If it was raining, the class would stay indoors and maybe read comics such as *Look and Learn*.

Many classes had a tuck shop, which was usually run by the well-behaved kids (the ones who could be trusted with the money!). Snacks that they sold included Smith's crisps, KP peanuts and Rich Tea biscuits. You could get eight Rich Tea biscuits for a penny, which perhaps doesn't sound very exciting nowadays. Cans of drink including orangeade and Coca-Cola were also sold, and the money raised went towards the school funds.

In longer dinner breaks, children would play football

and also games such as British Bulldog, and cowboys and Indians, or re-enact the Second World War. Marbles were played in the summer and conkers in the autumn. Every boy had a collection of conkers, and finding a horse chestnut tree was like finding the Holy Grail. Each conker would have a string fed through it and it was taken in turns to hit the other person's conker until one of the conkers broke. A point was given to the person with the surviving conker. Soaking a conker in vinegar would harden it and give it a better chance of winning. Older conkers were also harder so keeping one for a year gave a boy a better advantage the following year.

All boys played marbles and had their own collection, which they had either won or bought from the local sweet shop. Marbles could be bought in small bags for a couple of pennies. Some were prized more than others, depending on their size and colour. Depending on where you lived, ordinary-sized marbles were sometimes called 'alleys' and larger ones were called 'stumpers'. Large ball bearings were much sought after and were worth more when playing. To play, a shallow hole would be dug in the mud and players would compete against opponents until one had lost all his marbles. At the end of the term, the boy with the most marbles would often shout 'scrambles' and throw them one by one for other boys to run after and collect.

One of the most exciting games in the playground was British Bulldog. The game was extremely popular and consisted of two teams who stood on either sides of the playground. Kids would have to run from one end to the other and the boys in the middle had to try and catch them. It could get quite aggressive at times but no one came to much harm.

Occasionally, a fight would break out and everyone would gather around to cheer one side against the other. After a while, a dinner lady or teacher would break the fight up.

Bullying would sometimes take place. Having a girlfriend could be highly embarrassing for a boy, and even the suggestion would gather a crowd who followed the boy chanting 'so-and-so's got a girlfriend!' Most of the time it wasn't true.

Most children stayed at school for school dinners. Parents paid a fee for the dinners, which was approximately half a crown for the week. Long queues formed outside the dinner hall before the children were served. Menus included food like roast potatoes, carrots, sausages, meat (the cheap fatty cuts were used often) and for afters, spotted dick and custard or jam roly-poly. Some children loved school dinners and put their hands up for 'seconds' but many hated them. Children were told off for not finishing the food on their plates and if caught could get lines, detention or, in some cases, the cane. This meant that most children ate their school dinners whether they liked them or not. At Christmastime, a special Christmas meal would be put on. Some schools would have their own class parties complete with jelly and blancmange.

School trips were organised occasionally and usually involved a subject taught in class. Many trips were to historical locations such as National Trust properties or historical areas near to the school.

Before everyone broke up for the summer holidays, which caused much excitement, the school would organise its annual sports day. All children were expected to take part, and their parents would come to watch. Events included running, baton racing, high jump, long jump and swimming.

Each end of term brought a school report, which was handed to a pupil to give to his parents. The envelope came sealed but many children read theirs before they got home. The school report recorded how the child had done over the term. Few were glowing and many carried the sentence, 'Could do better!' Once parents had read the report, a slip at the bottom had to be signed by one of the parents to say that they'd seen it.

Schools would also have regular jumble sales and fêtes to raise money, usually just before the spring, summer and Christmas holidays. Children would be asked to donate something like old toys or comics and parents would be asked to donate tins of food and other items. Entry tickets were issued, and were sold, often by the pupils, to friends and relatives. Sometimes there was a prize for the pupil who sold the most. Jumble collections were also arranged and children knocked at doors asking for anything suitable.

During the harvest festival, parents were asked for tins of food, which were later donated to the local church to be distributed among the elderly.

Christmas was a great time in the classroom. Decorations would be made and games played on the last day of term. Some schools even allowed pupils to bring in a toy. Bible stories were read, which all added to the excitement of the occasion. Many children took part in the school nativity play and parents were asked to make costumes and were invited to watch. There were also organised carol services in the area and, if you were in the school choir, you were asked to sing at the local church.

Although teachers were still strict, many weren't as strict as the teachers had been in the 1950s. Classes were still well controlled, though, and unruly behaviour wasn't tolerated. Any misbehaving child would find themself facing the wall, with their hands on their heads or out in the hallway. Some would be sent to the headmaster's office to await the cane.

Homework included, to start off with, spelling, handwriting skills and learning fractions and multiplication tables. Tests, both written and verbal, would be held in the classroom the next day, with the teacher firing questions at his pupils, much to the embarrassment of many. One of the main tests of a pupil's ability came with the eleven-plus exam as children prepared to leave junior school. The exam decided which school they should attend after junior school and their abilities to cope with it. The exam included general knowledge, basic maths and English, as well as multiple-choice questions. Further exams came when pupils finally completed their school education. The legal school leaving age in the 1960s was just fifteen years old. The CSE (Certificate of Secondary Education) was introduced in the 1960s to provide a qualification for all school leavers. The GSE (General Certificate of Education or O level) was only taken by the minority of schoolchildren so many, previous to the CSE being introduced, left with no qualifications. The CSE was graded from 1 to 5. The highest grades were equivalent to O level passes.

Fridays would finish with an end of the week assembly, together with more prayers and hymns. An end-of-term assembly would also be held before school breaks. School holidays were much looked forward to by every child, and included three weeks off at Easter, six weeks off for the summer and three weeks off for Christmas.

A school day ended at 4 p.m. when all children rushed out of the classroom to get home as quickly as possible to watch their favourite television programmes and to have their tea and, if it was summer, to get out again quickly to meet their friends and play football or build dens. Many at the time couldn't wait to leave school, but today most people remember it as one of the best times of their lives.

6

Illnesses

A huge change took place in the 1960s after the development of polio vaccines. A feared illness in the 1950s and before, polio was now becoming less common. Mass immunisation using vaccines, developed by Albert Sabin and Jonas Salk, now brought what was once a dreaded illness under control. Albert Sabin developed an oral polio vaccine which was licensed in 1962. This type of polio vaccine was given with a lump of sugar.

Every child in a classroom in the 1960s ended up catching anything that was going around at the time. This included mumps, measles, German measles, colds and flu. Measles was very common and caused a fever, cough, runny nose and red eyes. This was soon followed by a rash. The illness was highly contagious. In the previous decade measles had killed hundreds of people in Britain. The worst epidemic was in 1941 when 1,145 died as a result of contracting the illness. Measles could also lead to loss of eyesight, and breathing and neurological problems. Vaccines for measles reduced the amount of reported cases greatly. A vaccine was developed by Maurice Ralph Hilleman, who also produced vaccines for mumps, hepatitis A, hepatitis B, chickenpox, meningitis, pneumonia and *Haemophilus influenzae*. By doing so, he saved millions of lives.

German measles (rubella) caused a rash, fever and swollen glands, and again easily spread in a 1960s classroom, which usually contained more than thirty children.

Mumps was another inevitable illness during childhood. It caused swelling to the face as well as fever and headaches. In children, it generally ran its course over several weeks without any major complications.

Chickenpox was yet another highly contagious disease spread by coughing and sneezing, and produced a rash, fever, headaches and aching muscles.

Meningitis was rare, but the airborne infection could be fatal to both children and young adults. Penicillin had some effect against the disease.

Many illnesses, such as stomach upsets, headaches and coughs and colds, led to days off school. Many kids were happy to have the time off and to be pampered by their mothers while they read comics or books. Doctors were happy to visit homes and often prescribed penicillin, which came in a pink liquid form. Doctors in the 1960s ran small surgeries, often from converted houses, and knew many of their patients by name.

Coughs, colds and flu seemed to be a lot worse for children, and many mothers rubbed Vicks VapoRub on their children's chests to relieve congestion and sinus problems. Cough syrups and sweets were used to ease the pain of a sore throat. There were many available, and all the products would be advertised on television when the season for getting colds and flu began.

Visitors to school included the nit nurse, who would comb children's hair in search of any foreign invaders. There would also be visits from opticians and hearing specialists. The optical test would involve reading from an eye chart and testing for colour blindness by making a child look at pictures made up of hundreds of coloured dots. If they could spot the number within the picture, their eyesight was fine, but if not, they were probably colour-blind. Kids with lazy eyes were given a pair of NHS glasses with a pink Elastoplast stuck over one lens. Hearing specialists examined ears and then spoke quietly behind a pupil to see if they could hear okay. Nurses also checked for flat feet and verrucas. A later test at school for boys involved them dropping their trousers and coughing. No one was ever quite sure what it was for though!

Besides being worn on NHS glasses, Elastoplasts were regularly used for grazed heads, cut knees and hands. Scraped knees were treated with iodine, which stung and also stained knees yellow. Bee and wasp stings were often soaked in Dettol, which was widely used as an antiseptic not only by mothers but by school dinner ladies and anyone else in charge of children.

Yearly checks with the school dentist were much feared. The dentist always found at least one tooth to drill and this he would do without anaesthetic. Any teeth that had to be taken out meant that the child would have to be given gas, which was administered with a rubber mask placed over the face. Lucky kids had parents with their own private dentists, which meant a visit to the school dentist was avoidable.

Tonsillitis was a very common condition for children during the 1960s and all suffering from it were taken into hospital to have their tonsils removed. The only benefit was that they were given ice cream after the operation.

Appendicitis was also common and meant a visit to the hospital for an operation. Many boys would return to school after having their appendixes out and proudly show off the scar.

The BCG (standing for Bacillus Calmette-Guérin) injection was given to all schoolchildren, and protected against tuberculosis. The programme was effective in eliminating TB in Britain, with new cases only reappearing here in recent years.

Common accidents involved falling off bikes, falling out of trees or falling off walls. Everything was seen as an adventure, and many boys somehow managed to split their heads open or break arms, and would end up at the X-ray department of the local hospital. There was always a kid in class who would have his arm in plaster, on which everyone would happily sign their name. Even the local playground could be a source of accidents, and many children were hurt by swings or see-saws. The concrete floors of playgrounds made the damage even worse, especially when children fell over or came off something.

Headaches always seemed worse as a child. Treatment included Alka-Seltzer tablets, which were dissolved in water. Their slogan was 'there's nothing like Alka-Seltzer for headaches and indigestion'.

There's no doubt that illnesses seemed a lot worse in childhood, but once an immunity was built up many illnesses such as measles and mumps were gone forever. An inevitable drawback to an adventurous outdoor life was the odd knock, bruise and broken limb but it all, somehow, seemed worth it!

7

Fashion

Fashion changed greatly over the 1960s. The beginning of the decade carried on fashions which had been popular in the 1950s. Later fashions included miniskirts and maxi skirts, hot pants, corduroys, snazzy shirts and winkle-picker shoes. Ladybird produced many fashionable clothes for children, which were small-scale versions of what their parents wore.

Fashions were altered by ideas coming from the London pop scene. Musical taste and fashion were closely linked and styles developed from rockers and mods to the clothes that defined a generation. By the middle of the 1960s, the A-line, flared at the bottom, was in fashion for skirts, dresses and coats. Later, fashions which featured well-fitting, brightly coloured outfits were seen mostly in boutiques in 'Swinging London'. These garments greatly influenced fashions all around the world. Men's suits became slimmer-fitting and were accessorised with bright-coloured shirts and ties. The jackets featured wider collars and the trousers were flared and worn together with high-heeled boots.

Designers used new materials such as PVC and Perspex to make coats and dresses. Paco Rabanne famously made dresses from plastic discs held together with metal links.

The hippy look came from the West Coast of America. For adults, the hippy influence produced tie-dye and batik fabrics, bell-bottoms and paisley prints. A famous quote from this movement was 'turn on, tune in, drop out', said by Timothy Leary at a meeting of 30,000 hippies in San Francisco in 1966.

Mary Quant introduced the miniskirt in 1964 and with it went matching hairstyles and huge false eyelashes. Carnaby Street and Chelsea's King's Road were seen as the places to be to see the latest fashions, and many people were influenced by the models of the day, including Twiggy, Jean Shrimpton, Colleen Corby, Penelope Tree and Veruschka. Photographers like Cecil Beaton, David Bailey and Richard Avedon produced iconic images that highlighted the fashions of the day.

Carnaby Street, by the 1960s, was famous for both mod and hippy fashion. Many designers and fashion boutiques were located there at the time, including Mary Quant, Lord John, Merc, Marion Foale and Sally Tuffin, Take Six and Irvine Sellars. Legendary bands including The Beatles, The Who, Small Faces and The Rolling Stones regularly shopped and socialised in the area and it became one of the coolest places in Swinging London in the 1960s.

There were many key figures who helped influence and capture the 1960s. These included Jean Shrimpton, who was an icon of Swinging London in the 1960s, with her face appearing on the covers of all the major magazines at the time, including *Elle, Glamour, Harper's Bazaar, Ladies' Home Journal, Newsweek, Time and Vanity Fair*. She began modelling in 1960 at the age of seventeen. *Glamour* named her Model of the Year in 1963. She was described, at the time, as the most photographed model in the world as well as having the world's most beautiful face. She was nicknamed The Shrimp and helped launch the miniskirt when she appeared at the Victoria Derby in Melbourne wearing a white dress, designed by Colin Rolfe, which ended 3½ inches above her knees. She was famously linked to David Bailey, and he was credited with having discovered her in 1960.

Twiggy was a model known for her thin build, large eyes, long eyelashes, and short hair. In 1966, she was named as The Face of 1966 by the *Daily Express* and also voted British Woman of the Year. By the following year, she had appeared on the covers of *Vogue* and *Tatler*, as well as modelling in Japan, France and the US, achieving worldwide fame. In January 1966, Twiggy, then still known as Lesley

Hornby, had her hair cut and coloured by celebrity hairstylist Leonard of Mayfair. The hairdresser had previously appealed for models so that he could try out his new crop haircut style. Photos were taken by professional photographer Barry Lategan and these were seen by Deirdre McSharry, a fashion journalist with the *Daily Express*. She asked to meet Lesley Hornby, and more photos were taken and featured in an article describing her as 'The Face of '66'. From then, her career took off and she was soon appearing in all the leading fashion magazines of the day. In 1967, she brought out her own fashion line called Twiggy Dresses. Her look became one of the iconic images of the 1960s.

David Bailey became the fashion photographer for British *Vogue* magazine at the beginning of the decade, and along with Terence Donovan and Brian Duffy helped to capture 'Swinging London' in the 1960s. The three photographers obtained celebrity status and associated with actors, musicians and royalty. The movie *Blowup* (1966), starring David Hemming, was based on David Bailey. Grace Coddington, the editor of American *Vogue*, said of Bailey,

> It was the Sixties, it was a raving time, and Bailey was unbelievably good-looking. He was everything that you wanted him to be – like the Beatles but accessible – and when he went on the market everyone went in. We were all killing ourselves to be his model, although he hooked up with Jean Shrimpton pretty quickly.

Bailey photographed all the major personalities of the day, including Mick Jagger, Terence Stamp, The Beatles, Andy Warhol and the Kray Twins. Rock photographers of the day not only photographed the stars but also captured many of the fashions of the 1960s. One of the best of these was Gered Mankowitz, whose photos of Jimi Hendrix, The Rolling Stones, Marianne Faithfull and Small Faces have an iconic appeal and have featured in endless magazines and on album covers.

With changing fashions came a new way of talking. New

words like fab and groovy entered the English language. Many new words seemed to appear during the hippy and psychedelic part of the 1960s although 'fab' appeared in the early 1960s in *Thunderbirds*, the Fab Four (The Beatles) and Fab 208 (Radio Luxembourg). Words like 'funky' are associated with the 1960s, but are much older and were used before the First World War. Something was good if it was a 'blast', a 'gas' or 'neat'. Terms of address for others included 'man', 'dude', 'cat' or 'chick'. 'Far out' meant awesome, 'hang loose' meant taking it easy, 'hip' meant very cool, 'heavy' meant serious, and a 'pad' was where you lived. Although there weren't many surfers in Britain at the time, surfing words included 'gnarly', which meant difficult, and 'wipe out', which meant to fall off a surfboard. There were many more. A lot of words disappeared for a long time but then seemed to come back into the English language, and many are still used.

The Summer of Love of 1967 popularised not only the hippy culture but also psychedelia, which, although associated with drugs, also greatly affected fashion at the time. Hypnotic designs and wild, vibrant colours featured in outlandish patterns on a whole manner of garments including kaftans, dresses, shirts and jackets. The Beatles helped promote the fashion, and psychedelic art also appeared on album covers (notably *Sgt Pepper's Lonely Hearts Club Band*), in paintings and on posters. Brightly coloured outfits, based on military uniforms, became common in fashion centres such as Carnaby Street.

Between 1966 and 1969, Zandra Rhodes and a fellow student at the Royal College of Art in London opened a boutique called the Fulham Road Clothes Shop. Her fellow student, Sylvia Ayton, designed the clothes while Rhodes provided the textile designs. In 1969, they went their own separate ways and Rhodes opened her own outlet in fashionable Fulham Road.

Mary Quant, together with Plunkett-Greene and a solicitor called Archie McNair, opened a small clothes shop called Bazaar on the King's Road during 1955. Good sellers were small, plastic white collars used to brighten up black dresses and T-shirts. In 1957, the trio opened a second branch of Bazaar. By 1966, Quant was designing and making most of the clothes she stocked rather than buying them from other companies. She became one of the key figures in fashion in the 1960s and took credit as one of the designers of the miniskirt and hot pants. Quant said of the miniskirt,

> It was the girls on the King's Road who invented the mini. I was making easy, youthful, simple clothes, in which you could move, in which you could run and jump and we would make them the length the customer wanted. I wore them very short and the customers would say, 'Shorter, shorter.'

The miniskirt was said to be named after Quant's favourite car at the time. By the late 1960s, after her association with the miniskirt and popularising hot pants, Quant had become a major British fashion icon.

In 1968, Sandie Shaw also started her own fashion label, producing her own brand of clothing and shoes.

The fashions of the day became apparent in many television programmes, such as *Department S*, in which they were worn by the flamboyant Jason King, played by Peter Wyngarde. The character would later become the inspiration for Austin Powers. Pop stars and television stars had a great influence on fashion. Watching *Top of the Pops* and other shows gave an idea of what the latest bands like The Who and The Kinks were wearing.

By the end of the decade, clothes were bright and colourful with many new styles that spilled over into the 1970s and beyond. The clothes of the 1960s changed fashion forever and many styles still remain fashionable today.

8

Music

Radio played a big part in many families' lives. In the early 1960s, in the days before Radio 1 and Radio 2, the BBC broadcasted the Light Programme. The service began in 1945 and continued until 1967 when it was renamed Radio 2.

Record Roundabout (1948–77) was hosted by bandleader Jack Jackson, and included recorded comedy in between music of the day. The lightning cutting between music and sketches was said to have given inspiration to DJs such as Kenny Everett.

Educating Archie (1950–61 and 1966) featured ventriloquist Peter Brough and his dummy Archie Andrews. It was broadcast every Sunday at lunchtime. During the 1950s, it had been one of the most popular radio shows to be broadcast and drew a huge audience. Regular guests on the show included Tony Hancock, Hattie Jacques and Peter Maddern.

Just Fancy (1951–62) featured character comedy from Kenneth Connor, Eric Barker and Deryck Guyler, who were resident comedians at the Cranbourne Towers Hotel. Unusually for the time, the show featured no studio audience.

The Clitheroe Kid (1957–72) featured the diminutive northern comedian Jimmy Clitheroe. In the show he played the part of a cheeky schoolboy who lived with his family at 33 Lilac Avenue. The show also featured Patricia Burke as his mother, Peter Sinclair as his Scottish granddad, Diana Day as his sister Susan (the part was also played by Judith Chalmers), Danny Ross as Alfie Hall (Susan's boyfriend) and

Tony Melody as Mr Higginbottom. Clitheroe was thirty-five when he first took the part but could pass for an eleven-year-old boy because of his small stature. When recording the show, Clitheroe would wear a school blazer and cap. The programme was immensely popular with radio listeners at the time.

Beyond Our Ken (1958–64) starred Kenneth Horne together with Kenneth Williams, Hugh Paddick, Betty Marsden and Bill Pertwee. The show's announcer was Douglas Smith. The scripts were written by Eric Merriman and Barry Took. The comedy series was a forerunner to *Round the Horne* (1965–68), which was written by Barry Took and Marty Feldman and featured sketches and musical interludes. Favourite characters in the show included Hankie Flowered (Bill Pertwee parodying Frankie Howerd), Betty Marsden's Fanny Haddock (based on Fanny Craddock) and Ricky Livid played by Hugh Paddick, who was sending up stars of the day such as Marty Wilde and Billy Fury.

Workers' Playtime (1941–64) was a variety show originally broadcast to boost workers' morale during the Second World War. It was initially broadcast on the BBC Home Service and later on the Light Programme. Many comedy and vocal artists appeared on the programme over the years, including Peter Sellers, Tony Hancock, Frankie Howerd, Terry Thomas and many more. The show toured the country visiting workers' canteens, bringing with them the best artists of the day to provide entertainment.

Paul Temple (1938–68) was originally created by author Francis Durbridge (1912–98) as part of the BBC radio serial *Send for Paul Temple*, which was first broadcast in 1938. An author of crime fiction, Temple is also an amateur private detective who solves whodunit-type crimes with his journalist wife, Steve. His wife gets her name from the pen name, Steve Trent, under which she writes. In 1969, the show transferred to television and Francis Matthews played the lead role.

Mrs Dale's Diary (1948–69) revolved around Mrs Mary Dale, who was a doctor's wife living at Virginia Lodge in the fictional middle-class area of Parkwood Hill. The main scriptwriter was Jonqil Antony, joined by Ted Willis who would later write for *Dixon of Dock Green*. Until 1963, Mrs Dale was played by Ellis Powell before she was replaced by Jessie Matthews. Each episode would begin with a brief narrative by Mrs Dale as if she were reading from her diary. The show became one of the BBC's most popular serial dramas.

The Archers (1951–present) was originally listed as 'an everyday story of country folk' and still continues today, making it the world's longest-running radio soap. Set in the fictional village of Ambridge, it tells the story of the middle-class farming family the Archers. It was first broadcast on Whit Monday on 29 May 1950, with five episodes being transmitted throughout the week. The pilot series, created by Godfrey Baseley, was described as 'a farming Dick Barton'.

Music While You Work (1940–67) was a live programme broadcast to entertain workers. The show began during wartime, and it was thought that continuously playing popular music would help factory workers become more productive. Originally, the show consisted of live music from bands playing brass, dance, military and light music.

Two-Way Family Favourites (1945–84) linked families at home with troops serving overseas in the forces. The show was hosted by husband-and-wife team Jean Metcalfe and Cliff Michelmore, and proved hugely popular. The forerunner of the show, *Forces Favourites*, was aired during the Second World War and featured requests, messages to loved ones, and music.

Housewives' Choice (1946–67) was a request show that played music that would appeal to housewives at home during the day. It featured mainly pop music of the day and achieved huge audiences. The theme tune was 'In the Party Mood' by Jack Strachey. There were various presenters but one of the most popular was George Elrick, who would sing his own lyrics over the theme song.

Blackpool Night (1948–63) was introduced by Gay Byrne and featured stars live from the resort, including Freddie Davies, Myrna Rose, Joe Kenyon, The Wedgewoods and 'Mr. Blackpool', Reginald Dixon, complete with the BBC Northern Dance Orchestra.

The Billy Cotton Band Show (1949–68) was broadcast on Sunday afternoons. Cotton would start the show by shouting, 'Wakey-Wake-aaaay!', which was followed by the song 'Somebody Stole My Gal', the band's signature tune. Regular entertainers on the show included pianist Russ Conway, Alan Breeze, Kathy Kay and Doreen Stephens. Michael Palin and Terry Jones wrote many jokes for the show.

Chapel in the Valley (1949–69) was a religious half-hour music programme introduced by Sandy McPherson, and featured vocals from Harvey Alan (who appeared as 'Mr Edwards') and organ music played by Charles Smart (who appeared as 'Mr Drewett').

Children's Favourites (1954–67) was first broadcast in 1954 and featured requests from children of all ages. It was broadcast on Sunday mornings at 9 a.m. and was introduced by Derek McCulloch, who was known as Uncle Mac. He opened the show with, 'Hello children, everywhere!' and ended it with 'Goodnight children, everywhere!', which became his catchphrase. The theme song to the show was 'Puffin' Billy', played by the Melodi Light Orchestra. Many children wrote in just to hear their names on the radio. McCulloch made his last broadcast in 1965 and eventually the show was renamed *Junior Choice*.

Saturday Club (1958–69) was hosted by Brian Matthew and was a two-hour 'experimental teenage music show' which followed on from a previous show in 1957 called *Skiffle Club*. The show included guest artists and live music. In 1967, Keith Skues took over the show when it was moved to the new Radio 1.

Sing Something Simple (1959–2001) featured melodies from the last seventy years sung by the Cliff Adams Singers, and was broadcast on Sunday evenings. It became the longest continuously running music programme in the world until it was axed in 2001.

Easy Beat (1959–67) was a mid-morning pop show broadcast on Sundays and hosted by Brian Matthew. It regularly featured Kenny Ball's Jazzmen, the Johnny Howard Band, Laura Lee, Tony Steven, Danny Street and many other guest artistes.

When it moved to Radio 1 in 1967, it was hosted by Keith Fordyce under the new title *Happening Sunday*, although it only lasted a few more months.

Enchanted Evenings (1964–65) featured music from stage and screen and was hosted by Bruce Trent.

Pick of the Pops (1955–72) was a popular chart show originally hosted by Franklin Engelmann, later followed by Alan Dell, David Jacobs and Don Moss. When it was moved to Sunday afternoons in 1962, it was hosted by Alan Freeman, who stayed in the job until 1972 when the show was renamed *Top 20*.

Semprini Serenade (1957–82) was a weekday show hosted by Alberto Semprini, who opened the show with the lines 'old ones, new ones, loved ones, neglected ones'. The show featured themes from films and stage shows as well as old and new tunes.

Your Hundred Best Tunes (1959–2007) was broadcast on Sunday evenings and was hosted by Alan Keith; it featured classic music.

Friday Night Is Music Night (1952–present) remains the world's longest-running live concert programme. It features a range of music, including classical, film, swing, jazz, opera, folk and songs from musicals.

Have a Go (1946–67) was hosted by Wilfred Pickles and featured the catchphrases 'how do, how are yer?', 'are yer courting?', 'what's on the table, Mabel?' and 'give him the money, Barney!' The series regularly attracted an audience of 20 million, and contestants could win £1 19s 11d by sharing their secrets.

Twenty Questions (1947–76) was originally hosted by Stewart MacPherson, who was later followed by Gilbert Harding and Kenneth Horne. Celebrity guests had to guess the identity of an object by asking twenty questions.

Listen with Mother (1950-82) was broadcast every weekday afternoon at 1.45 p.m. and lasted fifteen minutes. Its presenters included Daphne Oxenford, Eileen Brown, Julia Lang, Dorothy Smith and many others. It consisted of stories, nursery rhymes and songs which were regularly sung by Eileen Browne and George Dixon. The show was aimed at the under-fives, and regularly had over 1 million listeners. The theme tune was Gabriele Fauré's 'Dolly Suite', and the show began with the words 'are you sitting comfortably? Then I'll begin.' It led on to the television version, *Watch with Mother*.

Woman's Hour (1946–present) was hosted by Marjorie Anderson and Judith Chalmers during the 1960s, and featured items of interest to women, including interviews and topical debates. The show still continues today and attracts millions of listeners.

The Light Programme ceased on 30 September 1967 on the same day that Radio 1 commenced. The disc jockeys on Radio 1 were mainly culled from pirate stations such as *Radio Caroline* and *Radio London. Caroline* had broadcast out at sea, just outside British territorial waters, to avoid broadcasting laws. They first started broadcasting on 27 March 1964. In April 1964, *Radio Atlanta* followed suit, broadcasting from a former coaster, the MV *Mi Amigo*. Tony Benn, the British Postmaster General, introduced a Bill to Parliament which effectively outlawed pirate radio stations. Many of the best-remembered DJs of the 1960s began their careers on pirate radio, including Tony Blackburn, Emperor Rosko, John Peel, Johnnie Walker and Kenny Everett.

Radio Luxembourg had been a favourite for years. Broadcasting from Luxembourg to Ireland and Britain, the service began in 1933. Many loved tuning in at night when the reception was better, although it was still far from perfect. Many shows were recorded in London and broadcast from Luxembourg to avoid broadcasting legislation. There were lots of competitions and the station featured many of the day's favourite DJs, including Barry Alldis, Ted King, and Don Wardell. Many London-based DJs recorded their shows at Radio Luxembourg's studios at 38 Hertford Street in London. These included Peter Aldersley, Jack Jackson, and Muriel Young.

A typical week on Radio Luxembourg consisted of:

Sundays
6.00 p.m. – *Butlin's Beaver Club* with Uncle Eric Winstone.
8.30 p.m. – *Take Your Pick* with Michael Miles.

9.30 p.m. – *This I Believe*. The Edward R. Murrow show presented by Sir Basil Bartlett.

Mondays
9.30 p.m. – *Candid Microphone*, starring listeners caught in the act.
11.15 p.m. – *Frank and Ernest* – religion from the Dawn Bible Students Association.
11.30 p.m. – *The World Tomorrow* with Herbert W. Armstrong.

Tuesdays
9.00 p.m. – *Lucky Number* with Keith Fordyce.
10.00 p.m. – *The Capitol Show* – Mel Thompson presenting Capitol Records' new releases.

Wednesdays
8.00 p.m. – *Double Your Money* with Hughie Green.
10.00 p.m. – *Rockin' to Dreamland* with Keith Fordyce playing the latest British and American hit records.
11.30 p.m. – *The Hour of Decision* with Billy Graham.

Thursdays
8.30 p.m. – *Lucky Couple* with David Jacobs, recorded on location in the UK.
9.30 p.m. – *Irish Requests*.
10.45 p.m. – *Italy Sings* presented by the Italian State Tourist Office.

Fridays
10.30 p.m. – *Record Hop* – Benny Lee presenting the latest Columbia and Parlophone Records.

Saturdays
7.00 p.m. – *Amateur Football* – results of the matches played that day.
8.00 p.m. – *Jamboree* – 120 minutes of exciting, non-stop, action-packed radio ... *Teenage Jury* and at approximately

9.30 p.m. Alan Freed, the remarkable American disc jockey whose programmes in the States cause excitement to rise to a fever pitch, presented *Rock 'n' Roll*.

10.00 p.m. – *Tonight* – Peter Haigh presents news, music and personalities, recorded at the Embassy Club in London.

10.30 p.m. – *Philips' Fanfare* – records from this label, presented by Guy Standeven.

Radio Luxembourg is remembered for playing favourite hits and the songs that the BBC wouldn't play, but there was also a lot of religion thrown in.

With the opening of Radio 1, featuring the latest pop music, and Radio 2, aimed at a more mature audience, both in 1967, the older channels such as the Light Programme ceased to exist. Many programmes continued on the new stations but, with the popularity of television, would never draw the audiences that they once had. However, they still drew listeners in their millions, and Radio 1 went on to pave the way for all future radio stations featuring pop music.

Music changed greatly over the 1960s. The decade started off with hits from artists such as Lonnie Donegan singing 'My Old Man's a Dustman', Johnny Preston with 'Running Bear', Perry Como with 'Delaware' and Adam Faith with 'Poor Me'. The harder rock and roll of the late 1950s had mellowed and now included artists such as Billy Fury, Bobby Darin, Joe Brown and the Everly Brothers. Artists that fitted in well in the 1950s, and had appealed to a previous generation, were still featured in the 1960s, and included Max Bygraves, Russ Conway, Johnny Mathis, Ronnie Carroll and Frankie Laine.

Families, including teenagers, had more disposable income to buy the latest releases, which at the time came on vinyl 7-inch 45 rpm records. Most record stores had their own listening booths so that people could listen to their favourite tracks before buying them.

Many teenagers now had their own portable Dansette record players to listen to the latest hits as well as transistor radios and reel-to-reel tape recorders.

An early chart, from March 1960, featured:

1 'Poor Me' by Adam Faith
2 'Running Bear' by Johnny Preston
3 'Slowboat to China' by Emile Ford and the Checkmates
4 'Why' by Anthony Newley
5 'Summer Set' by Acker Bilk
6 'Pretty Blue Eyes' by Craig Douglas
7 'You Got What It Takes' by Marv Johnson
8 'Delaware' by Perry Como
9 'La Mer' by Bobby Darin
10 'Voice in the Wilderness' by Cliff Richard and the Shadows

The Beatles changed the face of popular music forever. Decca famously rejected them, saying, 'We don't like their sound, and guitar music is on the way out.' The band had formed in Liverpool in 1960 and included Paul McCartney, John Lennon, George Harrison and Ringo Starr. Their first hit 'Love Me Do' was released in late 1962 and they soon gained a huge following. Their debut album *Please Please Me* was released in March 1963. As their popularity spread, the group were pursued by fans wherever they went, leading to the newspapers of the time dubbing the phenomenon Beatlemania. The Beatles' fame spread worldwide and they sold millions of records. The band split up in 1970 after Paul McCartney announced that he was leaving the group on 10 April of that year.

The Mersey sound took over the world, and other bands from the same area who found fame at the time included Gerry and the Pacemakers, The Merseybeats and The Swinging Blue Jeans. Other popular British beat groups included The Dave Clark Five, The Hollies and The Zombies. All were hugely successful.

Gerry and the Pacemakers were formed by their lead singer, Gerry Marsden, in 1959. Like The Beatles, they were from Liverpool, were managed by Brian Epstein and recorded by George Martin. They were the first act to reach number one in the charts with all of their first three singles. Their three number ones were 'How Do You Do It?', 'I Like It' and

'You'll Never Walk Alone.' Other hits included 'I'm the One' and 'Ferry Cross the Mersey'.

Billy J. Kramer and the Dakotas were also managed by Brian Epstein and they recorded several Lennon and McCartney compositions. In 1963, they recorded The Beatles song 'Do You Want to Know a Secret' which went to number two in the singles chart. Their next single, 'Bad to Me', another Lennon and McCartney composition, went straight to number one. This led to appearances on television shows, including *Shindig!*, *Hullabaloo* and *The Ed Sullivan Show*. Their biggest hit, 'Little Children', was released the following year and also went straight to number one.

The Merseybeats, like The Beatles and Gerry and the Pacemakers, had previously performed live at Liverpool's Cavern Club. The group was founded by Tony Crane and Billy Kinsley. Their first hit single came in 1963 with 'It's Love That Really Counts'. This was followed in 1964 by their million-seller, 'I Think of You'. They toured Germany and the US in 1964 and also had their own Italian television show. Other hits included 'Wishin' and Hopin'', which was also recorded by Dusty Springfield in 1964, and 'Don't Turn Around'.

The Kinks were led by Ray Davies and formed part of the British invasion of the US in the 1960s. They are seen today as one of the most influential bands of the decade. Hits included 'You Really Got Me' (1964), 'Sunny Afternoon' (1966), and 'Death of a Clown' (1967). Other members of the band included Dave Davies, Pete Quaife and Mick Avory.

There were many other influential bands in the 1960s, including The Rolling Stones, The Who and The Yardbirds.

Top of the Pops was launched on 1 January 1964 and the top ten from that week was:

1 'I Want to Hold Your Hand' by The Beatles
2 'Glad All Over' by Dave Clark 5
3 'She Loves You' by The Beatles
4 'You Were Made for Me' by Freddie and the Dreamers
5 'Twenty Four Hours from Tulsa' by Gene Pitney

6 'I Only Want to Be with You' by Dusty Springfield

7 'Dominique' by The Singing Nun

8 'Maria Elena' by Los Indios Tabajaras

9 'Secret Love' by Kathy Kirby

10 'Don't Talk to Him' by Cliff Richard

Solo artists had huge success in the 1960s. Cliff Richard had been a huge star at the end of the 1950s as rock and roll emerged, and his music continued to chart throughout the 1960s and beyond. His hits during the 1960s included 'Theme for a Dream' (1960), 'Summer Holiday' (1962) and 'Congratulations' (1967). 'Congratulations' was the UK entry in the Eurovision Contest on 6 April 1968. It came second in the contest, but the record went straight to number one. Cliff Richard also appeared in a number of highly successful film musicals during the early 1960s. Although he had the new beat groups to contend with, he still continued to chart.

Adam Faith was one of the most charted acts of the 1960s. His hits during the decade included 'Poor Me' (1960), 'The First Time' (1963) and 'Message to Martha' (1964). By 1964, his hits slowly declined, due partly to the success of The Beatles, with some singles failing to chart at all. However, his popularity had been immense during the period 1958–1965. He appeared in several films and toured as the lead in the theatre production of *Billy Liar* in 1967.

Tom Jones had great success in the 1960s. He was born Thomas Jones Woodward in Pontypridd, Glamorgan. During 1963, he was the front man for a Welsh beat group, *Tommy Scott and the Senators*. While playing at the Top Hat in Cwmtillery, he was spotted by London-based manager Gordon Mills. Mills agreed to manage him and took him to London, changing his name to Tom Jones, after the character in the popular 1963 film of the same name. His first single, 'Chills and Fever', released in 1964, failed to chart, but his next record, 'It's Not Unusual', became an enormous hit after it was promoted by the pirate radio station Radio Caroline. One of his records, 'Thunderball', was the theme song to a James Bond movie, but only reached number 35 in the charts.

His bigger hits included 'What's New Pussycat' (1965) and 'Green, Green Grass of Home' (1966). He regularly appeared on television and guested on other people's shows as well as having his own show, *This is Tom Jones*, which was broadcast between 1969 and 1971. He travelled to Hollywood in 1965 where he met, and became friends with, Elvis Presley. He first performed in Las Vegas in 1967.

Engelbert Humperdinck found fame with 'Please Release Me' in 1967, and the song charted in the top ten on both sides of the Atlantic, reaching number one in the UK. He was managed by Gordon Mills, a former room-mate and the manager of Tom Jones. 'Please Release Me' kept The Beatles' 'Strawberry Fields Forever/Penny Lane' off the top of the charts. Humperdinck also had hits with 'The Last Waltz' and 'A Man Without Love' and had his own popular television programme, *The Engelbert Humperdinck Show*.

Ken Dodd was not only a popular comedian and television star but also had a string of hits in the 1960s, including 'Love is Like a Violin' (1960), 'Happiness' (1964), and 'Promises' (1966). His most famous catchphrase was 'how tickled I am'.

Helen Shapiro was fourteen years old when she had her first UK hit in 1961. The single 'Don't Treat Me Like a Child' went to number three in the charts. Two further singles in that year went to number one and included 'You Don't Know' and 'Walking Back to Happiness'. In 1962, she had hits with 'Tell Me What He Said' and 'Little Miss Lonely'. She was managed by Norrie Paramor and toured with The Beatles in 1963.

Cilla Black began her career in 1963, and her hits included 'Anyone Who Has a Heart' (1964) and 'You're My World' (1964), which both reached number one in the charts. Black was managed by Brian Epstein and, in 1963, was his only female client. He introduced her to George Martin, who signed her to Parlophone Records where she recorded her debut single, 'Love of the Loved', which was written by Lennon and McCartney. She appeared on ABC-TV's *Thank Your Lucky Stars*, but the record only managed to chart at thirty-five. Her second single, 'Anyone Who Has a Heart', which was a cover of a Burt Bacharach and Hal David composition, became an instant hit. During 1966, Black recorded the theme song to the hit movie *Alfie*. She appeared in her own television special, *Cilla at the Savoy*, and, after the death of Brian Epstein in 1967, also starred in the BBC television series *Cilla* in 1968. Paul McCartney wrote 'Step Inside Love' for her, which was featured as the theme to the show every week. The show ran until 1976 and featured major stars of the day including Tom Jones, Cliff Richard, Johnny Mathis, Matt Monro, Georgie Fame and Sacha Distel.

Lulu was signed to Decca Records when she was just fifteen years old and first charted with a cover version of the Isley Brothers' 'Shout'. In 1966, she toured Poland with The Hollies. After leaving Decca in 1966, she signed to Columbia, where she was produced by Mickie Most. She returned to the UK singles chart in 1967 with 'The Boat That I Row', which was written by Neil Diamond. Her debut film, *To Sir With Love*, was made in the same year and starred Sidney Poitier. She sang the theme to the movie, and the track went to number one in the US. However, in the UK, it appeared as a B-side to 'Let's Pretend', which reached number eleven. Lulu appeared in a successful BBC television series, *Three of a Kind*, in 1967, and was given her own television show in 1968 which ran until 1975.

Petula Clark's career began as a child, singing on BBC radio during the Second World War. She had success with hits sung in French during the 1950s, but found global success in the 1960s with tracks including 'Downtown', 'Colour My World' and 'Don't Sleep in the Subway'.

Sandie Shaw was born Sandra Ann Goodrich and was spotted at a charity concert by Adam Faith, who introduced her to his manager, Eve Taylor, who secured her a deal with Decca Records in 1964. Her first single, 'As Long as You're Happy Baby' failed to make the charts but her second, 'There's Always Something There to Remind Me', rose to number one in the singles chart in the autumn of 1964. Her next single, 'Girl Don't Come' (originally a B-side), reached number three in the UK charts and was her biggest hit in America. She regularly appeared on television music programmes of the day including *Top of the Pops*, *Ready, Steady, Go!* and *Thank*

Your Lucky Stars. In 1967, she became the first British act to win the Eurovision Song Contest, with 'Puppet on a String'. In 1968, she hosted her own television show, *The Sandie Shaw Supplement*.

Marianne Faithfull began her singing career in 1964, and was discovered by Andrew Loog Oldham when she attended a Rolling Stones launch party. Her first chart hit, 'As Tears Go By', was written by Mick Jagger, Keith Richards and Andrew Loog Oldham. Successful follow-up singles included 'This Little Bird', 'Summer Nights' and 'Come and Stay with Me'. In 1965, she married artist John Dunbar, whom she later left to live with Mick Jagger.

Dusty Springfield was one of the most successful British female singers of the 1960s, with numerous top ten hits both in the UK and the US. She became an icon of the Swinging Sixties with her trademark bouffant hair, eyeliner and evening gowns. Her solo career began in 1963 with 'I Only Want to Be with You'. Following hits included 'I Just Don't Know What to Do with Myself' (1964), 'You Don't Have to Say You Love Me' (1966) and 'Son of a Preacher Man' (1968).

Mary Hopkin found fame on the talent show *Opportunity Knocks*. Twiggy saw her on the show and suggested to Paul McCartney that he sign her to The Beatles' Apple record label. Her first single, 'Those Were the Days', went to number one in August 1968. Her follow-up single, 'Goodbye', also written by Paul McCartney, reached number two, and this was followed by 'Temma Harbour', which reached number six in 1970. In the same year, she represented the UK in the Eurovision Song Contest with 'Knock, Knock Who's There?' and came second to Dana.

An appearance on *Top of the Pops* or other music shows of the day guaranteed that a record would rise up the charts. Listening to Alan Freeman presenting *Pick of the Pops* on the radio on Sundays was a must. The countdown of the top twenty, and later the top thirty, gave you a chance to hear where your favourite record was in the charts. Those with reel-to-reel tape recorders could actually record the whole chart or just their favourite song.

The top hits of the 1960s were:

1 'She Loves You' by The Beatles
2 'I Want to Hold Your Hand' by The Beatles
3 'Tears' by Ken Dodd
4 'Can't Buy Me Love' by The Beatles
5 'I Feel Fine' by The Beatles
6 'The Carnival Is Over' by The Seekers
7 'Day Tripper/We Can Work It Out' by The Beatles
8 'Release Me' by Englebert Humperdinck
9 'It's Now or Never' by Elvis Presley
10 'Green Green Grass of Home' by Tom Jones

American bands also dominated the charts and summed up an era. These included The Monkees, The Beach Boys and The Doors. Iconic solo American artists in the 1960s included Jimi Hendrix, Johnny Cash and Frank Sinatra.

The 1960s contained a wide variety of different music including folk, surf music, rock, blues, soul, psychedelic, blues, pop and country and was a period that went on to influence the music of generations to come. Motown was huge during the decade, and some of the most successful acts were Diana Ross and the Supremes, Marvin Gaye and Stevie Wonder. Folk also played a big part with hits by Bob Dylan, Joan Baez and Joni Mitchell.

9

Holidays

School holidays were much looked forward to, especially at Easter, summer and Christmas. Most schools had three weeks off for Easter, and with it being spring, there were more opportunities to play outside, build dens, make go-karts or just get up to mischief. Summer holidays went on for six weeks and seemed endless when you were a child. On warm and sunny days, kicking a ball around, riding your bike or playing in the woods took up a lot of the time. Most families would plan their annual holiday for the summer, which might mean trips to the seaside or visiting relatives living elsewhere in the country.

Trips abroad were almost unheard of in the early 1960s, and a dream holiday for a child, at the time, was a week at Butlin's. Butlin's holiday camps were set up by Billy Butlin just before the Second World War but hit their peak in the 1950s and 1960s. A trip to Butlin's meant free goes on fairground rides such as the dodgems (everyone's favourites) and free entertainment, as well as boating lakes, roller rinks and amusement arcades. Every camp had their own Beaver Club, which children could join for a shilling. This would entitle them to a free badge and certificate as well as a card on their birthday. Families stayed in small chalets, with some having their own cooking facilities. The camp was run by friendly redcoats, who would make sure that everyone was having a good time and would also provide entertainment throughout the day and in the evenings.

Billy Butlin opened his first holiday camp at Skegness during the Easter holiday of 1936. It was a low-key affair and the accommodation was basic. There was no heating in the chalets and no hot water. Butlin guaranteed free entertainment to all of his campers, no matter what the English weather threw at them. As well as their accommodation, they had access to bars, dining halls and theatres. To keep out the cold, campers ate their breakfasts dressed in warm clothes and danced in their overcoats. As the first campers arrived, the camp was still incomplete and didn't have its own water supply. Water was discovered three weeks later, after many boreholes had been sunk on site. Previous to the camp opening, Butlin had taken out a half-page advert in the *Daily Express* offering accommodation, four meals a day and free entertainment. He was soon inundated with enquiries, and 500 campers were expected on the day of its opening. The first campers played table tennis while the building of the camp continued around them. Even with its teething problems, over half of the people who stayed the first week booked to stay again. The popularity of the camp led to another being built at Clacton in 1938, and the construction of a third camp at Filey began in 1939.

When the Second World War broke out, completion of the Filey camp was postponed, and both the camps at Skegness and Clacton were taken over for military use. The Admiralty asked Billy Butlin to build two more camps for them to be used by military personnel. These were constructed at Ayr in Scotland and at Pwllheli in Wales. Butlin deliberately built the camps to a design that would make it relatively easy to covert them into holiday resorts after the war. When the war was over, the Navy moved out of the camp at Ayr in 1946 and ownership reverted to Butlin, who quickly brought the camp up to holiday standard and opened it to the public the following year. When it opened, it could accommodate 2,000 visitors, but this later increased to over 5,000. The camp at Pwllheli opened in March 1947 and could eventually accommodate a total of 8,000 guests. Butlin went on to open a camp at Mosney in Ireland in 1948. Three more camps opened in the 1960s, and these included one at Bognor Regis in 1960, another at Minehead in 1962 and finally one at Barry Island in 1966.

A child visiting Butlin's for a week, during the 1960s, would return to school afterwards and be the envy of their friends.

With more families having cars, many holidays involved camping or towing a caravan. Caravan holidays were immensely popular, and very exciting for children. Many caravans were far from posh, had no toilets and some even had gas lights. Sites specially built for caravans were set up and some would include electric hook-ups although most campers wouldn't have had televisions or other electrical appliances that are around today. Volkswagen camper vans were much used in the 1960s and contained all that you needed for a holiday. They were popular with families and were also associated with the hippy generation.

Other family holidays involved a drive to the country or seaside. Some stayed in bed-and-breakfast accommodation, which often meant that they had to stay out all day and only return in the evening. Holiday camps appealed to many, because all-day entertainment was laid on and a whole holiday, if a family wished, could be spent within the camp.

Special organised bus trips would take people to the seaside and countryside, to holiday destinations such as Blackpool or Skegness. Both towns were geared towards holidaymakers, with amusement arcades for the kids, donkeys on the beach, Punch and Judy shows and plenty of fairground rides. Swimming and sunbathing added to the holiday, as did lots of ice cream and candy floss. Meals in a café or fish and chips eaten outdoors, wrapped in newspaper, made the holiday.

Later in the 1960s, package holidays abroad became more popular, but were out of the reach of many families, most of whom spent their free time holidaying in Britain.

During the summer holidays, and at other times, most towns would be visited by the fair. Children would nag their parents until they took them, and there would be much excitement and discussion with their pals the next day. Many exciting rides were included, such as the dodgems, the waltzer and the big wheel. If your dad was a sharpshooter, he could perhaps win you a goldfish or cuddly toy by firing an airgun at metal targets, which usually resembled ducks. There was a similar hoopla stall, but many prizes seemed impossible to win. The smell of the fair added to the experience and was a mixture of hot dogs (every kid had to have one), candy floss and, at night, kerosene heaters.

Local events during the summer holidays would include fêtes and jumble sales. School fêtes were much fun, with lots of competitions and events.

Christmas holidays were looked forward to very much. The thought of the Christmas season, with lots of presents and lots of good programmes on television, proved very exciting to children. The holiday usually lasted for three weeks, with the new term starting in January; every kid would chatter about what toys they'd got and what they'd been up to over the Christmas period. Even though there were shorter days, there was still much fun to be had.

There was much anticipation during the lead-up. Most children had their own advent calendars, which contained twenty-five doors, and one door was opened each day, beginning on 1 December. The pictures behind the doors contained images of things with a nativity-type feel, such as candles, holly and religious themes. Most advent calendars at the time featured the nativity scene, featuring the baby Jesus, behind the door of 25 December.

Children were more naive in the 1960s, and more believed that there actually was a Santa Claus. Every kid was thrilled at the thought of Father Christmas visiting on the night of the 24th, entering through the chimney and leaving presents. Many would write letters to Santa telling him what they would like for Christmas, and lots of children were taken to large department stores to visit the various Santas there, who were all dressed for the part and came complete with red robes and cotton wool beards. At home, children would leave biscuits and milk for Santa's reindeer on Christmas Eve.

Television advertising aimed at children really took off in the 1960s. As soon as it was 1 December, adverts featuring the latest toys would appear on the telly. Adverts featuring Action Man showed him having mock battles and getting up to all sorts of adventures, and Scalextric tracks looked like something out of Le Mans. Manufacturers all made sure that they did their best to get children to pester their parents for their products, and many campaigns were very successful. There seemed to be a craze for one particular toy every year. By 1969, that toy was the spacehopper which looked fantastic in adverts but wasn't quite as much fun in real life!

School life was also more exciting leading up towards Christmas. There was much fun thinking about soon being off school, as well as all the presents that were about to be received. As the day got nearer, classrooms would be festooned with decorations, many home-made. Coloured paper rings would be put together in class and hung from the ceiling. Cards for relatives and other decorations were also made. Every class would have an end of term Christmas party, which often included things like sausages on sticks and jelly and custard for afters. It was the one time of year that the school dinner ladies deviated from their usual school menu.

Children would be chosen to appear in the school nativity play, and costumes would be made by their mums. Many costumes involved a sheet and a tea towel to cover their kids' heads, but some could be quite inventive. Schools sold tickets for the nativity play which helped to raise funds and also probably paid for the school party.

Religion played a big part in the story of Christmas, and tales of the birth of Jesus would be read out in class. Traditional hymns would be sung, including 'Little Town of Bethlehem', 'Away in a Manger', and 'Once in Royal David's City'.

Some schools had their own group of children who would knock on doors and sing Christmas carols. More enterprising children did it off their own back and made themselves a few pennies into the bargain. Popular Christmas carols sung included 'The First Noel', 'The Holly and the Ivy', and 'Good King Wenceslas'.

Christmas cards would be exchanged with school pals

and other friends. Some schools would set up their own red postboxes, usually made out of a cardboard box and red crêpe paper, and pupils would deposit their Christmas cards in there ready to be handed out in the final week of term.

At home, much fun would be had putting up decorations and decorating the Christmas tree. By the 1960s, most families had an artificial tree, which would be covered in tinsel and electric fairy lights.

With the popularity of television, the new Christmas editions of the *Radio Times* and the *TV Times* were very much looked forward to. They covered the two weeks over the Christmas season and were much read by children looking for their favourite programmes and cartoons. All the best programmes and films seemed to be shown at Christmas, although many of the movies shown, such as *It's a Wonderful Life* or *Miracle on 34th Street*, dated back to the 1940s. Every well-loved show had its own Christmas special, and one of the most eagerly anticipated, by both adults and children, was *The Morecambe and Wise Show*. Children's shows such as *Blue Peter* showed children how to make nativity decorations like angels and fairies for the top of the tree. Most involved a discarded cardboard loo roll insert!

Tucked up in bed on Christmas Eve, there was much excitement as the wait for Santa began. Imaginations ran wild, and some children thought that they could hear the sleigh bells of Santa's sleigh as they slowly fell asleep. When they awoke the next morning, usually very early, many would find a stocking and presents at the end of their bed or under the tree, and would eagerly unwrap them before waking their parents, usually by jumping on them to show them what Santa had left (they already knew!).

As well as toys, many children received annuals of their favourite comics, cartoon characters or television stars. After playing with their toys, having breakfast and finally getting washed and dressed, all kids would be out on the streets on their new bikes, scooters or roller skates, or flying their Action Men through the air while girls pushed their new dolls in prams.

Other popular toys included the latest board games which would be played by the whole family after dinner.

Christmas dinner was a highlight, and anyone out playing would soon be called in. Dinner would involve roast turkey, or chicken, together with roast vegetables, stuffing and gravy. For afters, there would be a Christmas pudding – sometimes Dad would set it alight – which was served with custard. Some people baked sixpences into the Christmas pudding, which added to the excitement of eating it. There was much fun, if you didn't choke, finding a sixpence among your afters. If your relatives lived nearby, they would be invited too, and Christmas crackers would be pulled; wearing a coloured paper party hat was essential. All crackers came with little gifts, jokes or mottos, and reading them outloud all seemed part of Christmas.

After everyone was stuffed, the family would settle down to watch the television and enjoy the Christmas specials. By bedtime, it seemed very sad that it was all now over. However, there was still Boxing Day and almost another ten days of school holidays to look forward to!

Christmas in the 1960s was an exciting time when imaginations were allowed to run wild. Much of the fun came in actually believing there was a Father Christmas and, perhaps, a lot of the excitement has been lost over subsequent years.

10

Timeline

1960

On 13 February, France tested its first atomic bomb. Named *Gerboise Bleue*, the blast took place in the middle of the Algerian Sahara Desert.

The queen gave birth to Prince Andrew on 19 February.

On 3 March, Elvis Presley returned home after being on army duty in Germany for two years.

An iconic image of Che Guevara was taken by photographer Guerrillero Heroico in Havana during March. It would later appear on T-shirts and other products all over the world.

On 1 May, the Soviet Union shot down an American Lockheed U-2 spy plane. On board was Francis Gary Powers, a CIA agent, who was captured alive.

The satellite *Sputnik 4* was launched into orbit by the Soviet Union on 15 May.

To Kill a Mockingbird by Harper Lee was published on 11 July. It later won the Pulitzer Prize for the best American novel of 1960.

The first traffic wardens were deployed in London in September.

The cartoon *The Flintstones* debuts on ABC in America on 30 September. The show is best remembered for the exclamation 'Yabba Dabba Doo!'

Coronation Street first aired on 9 December.

The farthing was taken out of circulation on 31 December. A farthing was a quarter of a penny, and had been in circulation since 1714. It was introduced in the reign of Queen Anne. Many of the farthings used in the 1960s were produced in the reign of Queen Elizabeth, although older coins were still in circulation. Those minted in the reign of Elizabeth all dated from between 1953 and 1956, and the reverse featured a robin.

1961

John F. Kennedy became the 35th president of the United States on 20 January. He succeeded Dwight D. Eisenhower. Kennedy was forty-three at the time, and was the youngest man to have been elected to the office. He is famous for several speeches, including 'and so, my fellow Americans, ask not what your country can do for you; ask what you can do for your country'; 'ich bin ein Berliner' in West Berlin on 26 June 1963; and 'a man may die, nations may rise and fall, but an idea lives on'.

Edwin Bush became the first man to be caught by the police using the new Identikit system.

The Beatles performed for the first time at the Cavern Club in Liverpool on 21 March.

The Jaguar E-Type was first launched in April.

Yuri Gagarin became the first man in space on 12 April. Travelling in his Vostok spacecraft, he completed an orbit of the earth before returning home. He was much honoured, and received many titles and medals, including 'Hero of the Soviet Union'.

Alan Shepard became the first American in space on 5 May. Ten years later, he commanded the Apollo 14 mission to the moon. He became the fifth and oldest person to walk on the moon. He was forty-seven at the time of the moonwalk.

George Blake was sentenced to forty-two years in prison after being found guilty of spying for the Soviet Union.

The Berlin Wall was constructed by East Germany. Work commenced on 13 August and cut off West Berlin from East Berlin and East Germany. Guard towers were placed along the concrete walls and anyone trying to escape risked being shot. The wall remained in place until 1989.

1962

The BBC broadcast the first episode of *Z-Cars* on 2 January.

John Glenn became the first American to orbit the Earth on 20 February, flying the *Friendship 7*. He was the fifth person in space after cosmonauts Yuri Gagarin and Gherman Titov and the missions of fellow US astronauts Alan Shepard and Gus Grissom.

Panda crossings were introduced on 2 April, but their flashing lights confused both drivers and pedestrians.

AT&T's Telstar became the first communications satellite to be launched into space, on 10 July. It successfully relayed television pictures, telephone calls and fax images.

On 11 July, live television was first broadcast from America to Britain via the Telstar satellite.

In October, The Beatles had their first hit with 'Love Me Do', which reached number seventeen on the *Record Retailer* chart. The record was recorded at the EMI studios in London and appeared on the Parlophone label.

The first live transatlantic television was broadcast via the Telstar Satellite on 23 July. The broadcast featured Walter Cronkite and Chet Huntley in New York with the BBC's Richard Dimbleby in Brussels. The broadcast included pictures of the Statue of Liberty in New York and the Eiffel Tower in Paris.

Marilyn Monroe was found dead on 5 August. Her death was recorded as 'probable suicide', although it was thought that the overdose may have been accidental. She was well known for her famous quote: 'What do I wear in bed? Why, Chanel No 5, of course.'

The first audio cassette was invented in 1962. By the 1970s, the cassette proved strong competition for the vinyl LP, and most homes had their own cassette player.

1963

The Beatles had their first number one hit with 'Please Please Me' in January. Their first album, also called *Please Please Me*, was released on 22 March. The album featured the tracks 'I Saw Her Standing There', 'PS I Love You', and 'Twist and Shout'.

On 5 March, country singer Patsy Cline was killed in a plane crash while returning from a benefit gig in Kansas.

Alcatraz prison closed on 21 March, and the last twenty-seven prisoners were transferred elsewhere.

Dr No was released in US cinemas during May and became the first of many James Bond movies. During the 1960s, the series starred Sean Connery and George Lazenby. Connery appeared as James Bond in *Dr No*, *From Russia with Love*, *Goldfinger*, *Thunderball* and *You Only Live Twice*. George Lazenby took over the role for one film, *On Her Majesty's Secret Service*, in 1969.

The movie *Cleopatra* was released on 12 June. It starred Elizabeth Taylor and Richard Burton.

On 16 June, Soviet cosmonaut Valentina Tereshkova became the first woman to travel into space, on board Vostok 6. She returned to Earth three days later.

The Great Train Robbery took place in Buckinghamshire on 8 August. The gang got away with £2.6 million, most of which was never recovered. The fifteen-strong gang was led by Bruce Reynolds, and included Gordon Goody, Buster Edwards, Charlie Wilson, Roy James, John Daly, Jimmy White, Ronnie Biggs, Tommy Wisbey, Jim Hussey, Bob Welch and Roger Cordrey. Three other men, known only as '1', '2' and '3', and an unnamed retired train driver were also present at the time of the robbery. The gang hid out at Leatherslade Farm, and incriminating evidence found there led to the eventual arrest and conviction of most of the members of the group. The ringleaders were later each sentenced to thirty years in jail.

Martin Luther King delivered his famous speech featuring the words 'I have a dream' on the steps of the Lincoln Memorial on 28 August.

The Lamborghini car manufacturing company was founded in Italy on 30 October.

John F. Kennedy was assassinated while visiting Dallas in Texas on 22 November. He was mourned all around the world. His killer, Lee Harvey Oswald, was later shot by Jack Ruby.

Doctor Who was first broadcast on 23 November. It starred William Hartnell as the Doctor, and his first adventure, called 'An Unearthly Child', took him and his granddaughter, Susan, back to the Stone Age. The introduction of the Daleks in the second series of episodes made the show an instant hit. Daleks suddenly appeared everywhere, including in comics, as toys, and on ice lollies. In 1966, the Doctor regenerated, and for the following three years was played by Patrick Troughton.

1964

The Beatles arrived at JFK international airport in February and were met by thousands of fans, marking the first occasion of Beatlemania in America. They later appeared several times on the *Ed Sullivan Show*, which cemented their popularity in the US. On arriving in America, Ringo Starr said, 'So this is America. They must be out of their minds,' and George Harrison asked, 'America has everything, why should they want us?'

Cassius Clay beat Sonny Liston to be crowned Heavyweight Champion of the World in Florida on 25 February.

On 15 March, Elizabeth Taylor and Richard Burton married for the first time. Their marriage lasted until 1974. They were married again in 1975 and the marriage lasted until 1976.

On 29 March, Radio Caroline became the first pirate station to broadcast to the mainland from a ship anchored outside Britain's territorial waters. The MV *Caroline* was anchored off Felixstowe and began test transmissions on 27 March. It was opened by Simon Dee, and the first programme broadcast was a pre-recorded show hosted by Chris Moore. The station's slogan was 'your all-day music station'.

On 4 April, The Beatles held the top five positions in the US Billboard chart with 'Can't Buy Me Love', 'Twist and Shout',

'She Loves You', 'I Want to Hold Your Hand' and 'Please Please Me'.

On 16 April, the Rolling Stones released their first album. Entitled *The Rolling Stones*, it appeared on the Decca label and included the tracks 'Route 66', 'Mona (I Need You Baby)', and 'You Can Make It If You Try'.

The Kinks' first album was released on 2 October. Entitled *Kinks* in the UK, the album had a different title in the US, where it was called *You Really Got Me*. The UK album featured the tracks 'Beautiful Delilah', 'You Really Got Me', and 'Got Love If You Want It'.

On 8 April, the unmanned Gemini 1 was launched. The mission was a test flight and lasted four hours and fifty minutes.

BBC Two was first broadcast on 20 April. It was the third British television station to be launched. *Play School* became the first programme to be shown the following morning. The launch had been intended to include more highbrow television, ending with a grand firework display but a huge power failure meant that this wasn't broadcast.

On 12 June, Nelson Mandela was sentenced to life imprisonment in South Africa. He spent the years 1964 to 1982 in prison on Robben Island. Mandela was finally freed in 1990 and became the first president of South Africa in 1994.

On 31 July, Ranger 7 sent back the first close-up pictures of the Moon. The craft became the first successful flight of the Ranger program, although it later impacted with the Moon.

On 27 August, Walt Disney's *Mary Poppins* was released in America. It starred Julie Andrews and Dick Van Dyke, and was a huge box-office success.

On 17 September, *Goldfinger* was first released. The movie was incredibly popular, both with adults and children, and introduced the classic Bond car, the Aston Martin DB5. Villains in the movie included Auric Goldfinger and his Korean manservant Oddjob.

Bewitched was aired for the first time in America on 17 September. The comedy told the story of a witch married to a mortal man and her use of her magic powers to get them out of various scrapes. It starred Elizabeth Montgomery as Samantha, Dick York as Darrin (her husband) and Agnes Moorehead as Endora. In 1969, Dick Sargent took over the role of Darrin.

On 14 October, Martin Luther King won the Nobel Peace Prize. It was given to him for combating racial inequality without using violence. The previous year, he had given a speech in St Louis, saying, 'We must learn to live together as brothers or perish together as fools.'

On 16 October, Harold Wilson became the prime minister of Great Britain. He became the leader of the Labour Party in 1963 after the sudden death of Hugh Gaitskell. He remained in the position until 1970 and was re-elected in 1974.

Wonderful Radio London began transmitting from a ship anchored off the south coast of England on 23 December. *The Fab 40* was transmitted from the MV *Galaxy*, which had formerly been a Second World War minesweeper. Most programmes were broadcast live from onboard the ship.

1965

Winston Churchill died on 24 January. He had previously served as prime minister during the war years between 1940 and 1945 and was later re-elected in 1951, serving until 1955. He was given a state funeral which was said to have been the largest in world history at that time.

Stanley Matthews played his final First Division football game on 6 February at the age of fifty years and five days.

The Sound of Music opened in New York on 2 March. It featured the music of Richard Rodgers and the lyrics of Oscar Hammerstein II, and was based on Maria Von Trapp's autobiography, *The Story of the Trapp Family Singers*. The film starred Julie Andrews and Christopher Plummer.

Cosmonaut Aleksei Leonov became the first man to walk in space on 18 March. The spacewalk lasted for twelve minutes. He was later selected to be the first Soviet man to land on the Moon but this mission was cancelled.

Astronaut Edward Higgins White made the first American spacewalk on 3 June. He later died during pre-launch testing of Apollo 1, the first manned Apollo mission, in a cabin fire. His fellow astronauts Virgil 'Gus' Grisson and Roger B. Chaffee also died.

Ronnie Biggs, one of the Great Train Robbers, escaped from Wandsworth prison on the 8 July.

Cigarette advertising was banned on British television on 1 August although cigars, such as Hamlet, continued to appear. Cigarette adverts continued to be shown in the cinema.

The Tom and Jerry cartoon series made its first appearance on US television on 25 September. The characters and cartoons, which dated back to 1940, were previously only seen in the cinema.

1966

Indira Gandhi was elected prime minister of India on 24 January. She stayed in the position until 1977, and was re-elected in 1980 before being assassinated in 1984.

The Soviet Luna 9 became the first controlled rocket-assisted spacecraft to land on the Moon. It also became the first vehicle to transmit photographic data from the surface. Luna 9 was the twelfth attempt by the Soviet Union to land a spacecraft on the moon.

The Labour Party, led by Harold Wilson, won the general election on 31 March. They won by a ninety-six-seat majority.

A regular hovercraft service began across the English Channel on 30 April. The service was run by Hoverlloyd, who operated between Ramsgate harbour and Calais. Townsend Ferries also ran a service from Dover to Calais, but that was soon superseded by Seaspeed, which was a joint operation between British Rail and France's Société Nationale des Chemins de Fer Français (the French National Railway Company).

Swinging Radio England and Britain Radio commenced broadcasting on 3 May from a ship anchored off the south coast of England.

Pet Sounds was released by The Beach Boys on 16 May. It was the eleventh album released by the group and featured the tracks 'Wouldn't It Be Nice', 'Sloop John B', and 'Caroline, No'.

The FIFA World Cup trophy was stolen on 20 June and was found, wrapped in newspaper, seven days later by a dog called Pickles. The police had previously been contacted and asked for a ransom of £15,000. When England won the World Cup, Pickles was invited to the celebrations, and his owner, David Corbett, received a reward of £6,000. Pickles appeared in a film called *The Spy with the Cold Nose*, starring Eric Sykes and June Whitfield, in 1966. He died a year later after choking on his lead while chasing a cat.

England won the World Cup after beating West Germany 4-2 on 30 July. The team was led by Bobby Moore, and the English goals were scored by Geoff Hurst and Martin Peters.

Hurst scored a hat-trick, which made him the only player ever to score three goals in a World Cup final.

Star Trek made its debut on 8 September in America, and featured Kirk, Spock, Scotty, McCoy, Sulu and Uhura on their five-year mission 'to boldly go where no man has gone before'. The show, starring William Shatner, became immensely popular all over the world.

Patrick Troughton took over the role of Doctor Who from William Hartnell on 29 October. He was seen as quite different from the previous Doctor, and said he played the role as a 'cosmic hobo'. The part soon became his, and the show became even more popular. He played the Doctor until 1970, when Jon Pertwee took over.

Walt Disney died while producing *The Jungle Book* on 15 December. The movie went on to be a huge success and the well-loved music track included 'The Bare Necessities', 'I Wanna Be Like You', 'That's What Friends Are For'. Children loved the weird and wonderful characters who featured in the film, including Mowgli, Baloo, Bagheera, King Louie, Shere Khan and Kaa.

1967

The Doors' debut album was released on 4 January.

US astronauts Gus Grissom, Edward Higgins White and Roger Chaffee were killed when fire broke out during a launch pad test of Apollo 1 on 27 January.

'Puppet on a String', sung by Sandie Shaw, won the Eurovision Song Contest on 8 April. The contest had ran since 1956, and Sandie Shaw was the first artist to win the contest for Britain. The song topped the UK singles chart on 27 April and stayed there for three weeks.

The Surveyor 3 probe landed safely on the moon on 20 April.

Vladimir Komarov became the first Soviet cosmonaut to die, due to the parachute on his space capsule failing when he returned to Earth on 24 April.

On 28 April, Muhammad Ali refused to enter military service, and was stripped of his boxing title and banned from fighting for three years.

Elvis Presley married Priscilla Beaulieu in Las Vegas on 1 May. Their marriage lasted until 1973 and they had one daughter, Lisa Marie, born in 1968. Presley died in 1977.

The Monterey Pop Festival began on 16 June and featured The Jimi Hendrix Experience, The Who, Ravi Shankar, Janis Joplin and Otis Redding. It was regarded as the beginning of the 'Summer of Love'.

BBC Two became the first UK channel to broadcast in colour on 1 July. By 1968, nearly every show on BBC Two was shown in colour. However, the vast majority of viewers still had black-and-white sets. BBC One started transmitting in colour six months later.

Brian Epstein, the manager of The Beatles, was found dead in his bedroom on 27 August. He was thirty-two years old. He had discovered The Beatles in 1961 while visiting Liverpool's Cavern Club during his lunch hour. Epstein had secured a meeting with George Martin, who then agreed to sign them to EMI's Parlophone label.

The BBC's Light Programme was split in two and became Radio 1 and Radio 2 on 30 September. The Light Programme had broadcast since 1945. Notable programmes included *The Archers*, *Educating Archie* and *The Goon Show*.

On 8 October, guerrilla leader Che Guevara was captured in Bolivia and executed the next day.

On 18 October, Walt Disney's *The Jungle Book* was released and became a huge box-office success.

The first *Saturn V* rocket was launched by the US on 9 November. On board was the unmanned *Apollo 4* test spacecraft.

The first heart transplant took place on 3 December. It was performed by South African cardiac surgeon Christiaan Barnard. The recipient was Louis Washkansky, who died eighteen days later of pneumonia caused by a weakened immune system.

On 31 December, Evel Knievel attempted to jump 141 feet over the fountains at Caesars Palace in Las Vegas. He crashed on landing and suffered many fractures as well as a crushed pelvis.

1968

In January, the Ford Escort was first introduced. It replaced the popular Ford Anglia.

2001: A Space Odyssey premiered in America on 2 April. It was directed by Stanley Kubrick. The film was partially based on Arthur C. Clarke's short story *The Sentinel*.

Planet of the Apes, starring Charlton Heston, was released on 3 April. It led on to four sequels, concluding with *Battle for the Planet of the Apes*. The make-up was revolutionary at the time.

Martin Luther King was shot dead in Memphis, Tennessee, on 4 April. Riots followed in many US cities. James Earl Ray was convicted of killing King, but protested his innocence.

Five- and ten-pence coins were introduced in April in the run-up to decimalisation, which was due to take place in 1971.

Robert F. Kennedy was assassinated in Los Angeles on 5 June. His assassin, Sirhan Sirhan, was later sentenced to life imprisonment.

The BBC comedy *Dad's Army* was first aired on the BBC on 31 July. Famous lines include 'Don't panic! Don't panic!' and 'We're doomed!'

The first Isle of Wight Festival was held on the 31 August. It featured Jefferson Airplane, Arthur Brown, The Move, Smile, Tyrannosaurus Rex, Plastic Penny and The Pretty Things.

'The White Album' was released by The Beatles on 22 November. It was the group's ninth studio album, and its proper title was *The Beatles*, but it became more commonly known as 'The White Album' because of its plain packaging. The album received mixed reviews, but contained many memorable tracks, including 'Back in the USSR', 'While My Guitar Gently Weeps', and 'Blackbird'.

Mattel's Hot Wheels toy cars were released on 6 September, and became immensely popular with children all around the world.

The television detective show *Hawaii Five-0* debuted in America on 20 September. It starred Jack Lord as Detective Lieutenant Steve McGarrett and James MacArthur as Detective Daniel 'Danno' Williams.

NASA launched the first manned Apollo mission, Apollo 7, and the first live broadcast from orbit took place. On board were astronauts Walter M. Schirra, Donn F. Eisele and R. Walter Cunningham. The mission lasted eleven days.

1969

On 16 January, two cosmonauts, engineers Aleksei Yeliseyev

and Yevgeny Khrunov, left Soyuz 5 for Soyuz 4 and became the first men to transfer between two spacecraft while in orbit.

Richard Nixon became 37th president of the United States on 20 January. He stayed in office until August 1974 when he resigned due to the Watergate scandal.

The Beatles gave their last public performance on the roof of Apple Records on 30 January as many spectators watched on. The impromptu concert went on for forty-two minutes, until the police put a stop to it. The event was filmed and later appeared in the documentary film, *Let It Be*, which was released in 1970. In the same year, George Harrison said, 'I can see the Beatles sticking together forever, really. We've been together a long time.'

The Boeing 747 made its maiden flight on 9 February.

Concorde made its first test flight on 2 March. It was retired from service in November 2003.

Apollo 9 was launched to test the Lunar Module on 3 March. The crew consisted of Commander James McDivitt, Command Module Pilot David Scott and Lunar Module Pilot Rusty Schweickart.

Golda Meir became the first female prime minister of Israel on 17 March. She remained in office until June 1974.

John Lennon and Yoko Ono married in Gibraltar on 20 March. They spent their honeymoon at the Hilton in Amsterdam, where they staged their week-long 'Bed-In for Peace'.

Robert Knox-Johnston became the first man to sail around the world single-handed on 22 April when he landed at Falmouth. He had previously left the port on 14 June 1968 in his boat *Suhaili*, which measured 32 feet. For his achievement, he was awarded the CBE (Commander of the Order of the British Empire).

Apollo 10 was launched on 18 May as a rehearsal for the moon landing. The mission tested all the procedures needed to get to the Moon without actually landing on it. The mission was crewed by Thomas P. Stafford, John W. Young and Eugene A. Cernan.

Judy Garland died of a drug overdose on 22 June. She was found dead in the bathroom of her rented home in Chelsea, London. Her death was recorded as 'accidental'.

Charles became the Prince of Wales at Caernarfon on 1 July. He was crowned by his mother, Queen Elizabeth II, in a televised ceremony.

Brian Jones, the original leader of The Rolling Stones, drowned in a swimming pool at his home in Sussex on 3 July. He was twenty-seven. Two days later, on 5 July, The Rolling Stones performed a free concert at Hyde Park.

US troops began to withdraw from Vietnam on 8 July.

Apollo 11 lifted off for the Moon on 16 July. On board were Neil Armstrong, Buzz Aldrin and Michael Collins.

The lunar module *Eagle* landed on the surface of the Moon on 20 July. Approximately 500 million people worldwide watched the live broadcast of Neil Armstrong taking the first steps on the Moon.

The Apollo 11 astronauts returned safely from the Moon on 24 July. On 11 August, they took part in a parade through New York, Chicago, and Los Angeles. President Nixon awarded each astronaut the Presidential Medal of Freedom.

The halfpenny ceased to be legal tender in Great Britain on 31 July. From 1717 to 1936, it had featured an image of Britannia on the reverse but thereafter, an image of the *Golden Hind* appeared on the back.

The Beatles were photographed by Iain Macmillan on the zebra crossing at Abbey Road on 8 August. The iconic image later appeared on their eleventh studio album, *Abbey Road*. The appearance of Paul McCartney on the cover barefooted led to rumours that he had died, to which he responded, 'I am alive and well and unconcerned about the rumours of my death. But if I were dead, I would be the last to know.'

The first ever episode of *Scooby-Doo, Where Are You* was broadcast in the US on 13 September. It soon became a favourite cartoon with children all over the world and led to many follow-up series.

Monty Python's Flying Circus was first aired on BBC Two on 5 October. The show ran until 1974. The team was made up of John Cleese, Michael Palin, Graham Chapman, Terry Jones and Terry Gilliam (who drew the animated scenes). Famous sketches included the parrot sketch, the nudge, nudge sketch, the lumberjack song and the Spanish Inquisition sketch. One of the best-remembered quotes was 'and now for something completely different', which had originally been used by Christopher Trace in *Blue Peter*.

On 26 October, The Beatles visited Buckingham Palace to be awarded MBEs by the queen. They arrived in John Lennon's Rolls-Royce and the police had to hold back 4,000 fans who had come to see them.

Regular colour broadcasts began on BBC One and ITV on 15 November. The BBC had previously announced that there would be a supplementary licence fee for anyone with a colour television, although the programmes could still be watched on black-and-white sets.

Sesame Street was first broadcast in the US on 10 November. Popular characters included Bert and Ernie, Big Bird, Elmo, Oscar, Kermit the Frog and the Cookie Monster. Jim Henson's

Muppets would later have their own show, which spawned movies and further television series.

Apollo 12, the second mission to the Moon, was launched on 14 November. On board were astronauts Pete Conrad, Richard Gordon and Alan Bean. The mission landed on the Moon on 19 November. When Conrad stepped on the moon, his first words were, 'Whoopie! Man, that may have been a small one for Neil, but that's a long one for me.' The mission carried the first colour camera but it was destroyed when Alan Bean accidentally pointed it at the sun.

Pelé scored his 1,000th goal on 19 November. The goal was scored at the Maracanã stadium in a match played against Vasco Da Gama. Pelé scored from a penalty shot. The goal became popularly known as *O Milésimo* (The Thousandth).

The Apollo 12 mission arrived safely back on Earth on 24 November. The crew and capsule were recovered by the USS *Hornet* before being flown to Pago Pago international airport for a reception. The next successful moon landing was on 9 February 1971.

John Lennon returned his MBE as a protest against Britain's involvement in the Nigerian Civil War. In an accompanying letter, he wrote, 'Your Majesty, I am returning my MBE as a protest against Britain's involvement in the Nigeria-Biafra thing, against our support of America in Vietnam and against "Cold Turkey" slipping down the charts. With Love, John Lennon.'

11

Memorable Personalities

Buzz Aldrin (born 20 January 1930)
Buzz Aldrin was the second man to walk on the Moon as part of the Apollo 11 mission. He set foot on the Moon on 21 July 1969 following fellow astronaut Neil Armstrong, and his first words on setting foot were 'beautiful view. Magnificent desolation.' He had formerly been a fighter pilot and became part of the space programme in October 1963.

Muhammad Ali (born 17 January 1942)
Muhammad Ali was born Cassius Marcellus Clay, Jr, but changed his name in 1964 after joining the Nation of Islam. He is considered one of the greatest heavyweights in boxing history. His looks, quick wit and character made him one of the sport's best-loved personalities. As Cassius Clay, he famously beat the reigning heavyweight champion, Sonny Liston, on 25 February 1964. Before the fight, he said, 'After I beat him I'm going to donate him to the zoo.' He also first uttered the phrase that would always be associated with him: 'float like a butterfly and sting like a bee!' In 1967, Ali refused to be conscripted into the US military and was stripped of his boxing title. He was also famous for the following quotes: 'I am the greatest!'; 'Cassius Clay is a slave name. I didn't choose it and I don't want it. I am Muhammad Ali, a free name – it means beloved of God, and I insist people use it when people speak to me and of me.'; and 'What's my name, fool? What's my name?',

addressed to Ernie Terrell, who refused to recognise his name change.

Arthur Askey (6 June 1900 – 16 November 1982)

Arthur Askey was an actor and comedian who found fame in the 1940s in films such as *Band Waggon* (1940), *The Ghost Train* (1941) and *I Thank You* (1941). By the 1950s, he was a household name, appearing on television in *Before Your Very Eyes!* in 1952. In 1957, he also appeared in *Living It Up*, a sitcom based on the *Band Waggon* format, which also starred Richard Murdoch. He had many catchphrases, including, 'Hello playmates!', 'Before your very eyes' and 'I thank you!' He continued to appear regularly on British television, particularly on panel shows. By the 1970s, he was a regular judge on the ITV show *New Faces*.

Gordon Banks (born 30 December 1937)

Gordon Banks was the goalkeeper in the 1966 England football team that went on to win the World Cup. He made 628 appearances during his fifteen-year career and won seventy-three caps. He was named footballer of the year in 1972 and was voted goalkeeper of the year on six occasions.

Brigitte Bardot (born 28 September 1934)

Brigitte Bardot was a film star and sex symbol throughout the 1950s and 1960s. She became world famous in 1957 after she appeared in the film *And God Created Woman*. Her face adorned many magazines throughout the 1960s, and she also released several albums and singles.

The Beach Boys

The Beach Boys music summed up the surf generation of the 1960s. Their popular hits included 'Surfin' USA' (1963), 'Fun, Fun, Fun' (1963), and 'California Girls' (1965). They are seen as one of the most influential American bands of the 1960s.

Christiaan Barnard (8 November 1922 – 2 September 2001)

Christiaan Barnard was the first person to perform a successful heart transplant operation. The procedure took place on 3 December 1967, lasted nine hours and involved a team of thirty people. His patient was Louis Washkansky, a fifty-four-year-old grocer who was already suffering from incurable heart disease. Barnard said afterwards that Washkansky was happy to take part in the operation. Barnard was later quoted as saying, 'For a dying man it is not a difficult decision because he knows he is at the end. If a lion chases you to the bank of a river filled with crocodiles, you will leap into the water, convinced you have a chance to swim to the other side.' Washkansky died eighteen days later because of a weakened immune system.

George Best (22 May 1946 – 25 November 2005)

George Best was born in Belfast and played as a winger for Manchester United as well as the Northern Ireland national team. The Irish Football Association described him as 'the greatest player to ever pull on the green shirt of Northern Ireland'. His talent and charisma made him one of the first celebrity footballers, and he lived a playboy lifestyle, dating Susan George, Barbara Windsor, Annette André and, later, Carolyn Moore, Miss Great Britain 1971. Pelé called Best the greatest player ever.

Tony Blackburn (born 29 January 1943)

Tony Blackburn was the first person to be heard on Radio 1 on 30 September 1967. He had previously been a disc jockey broadcasting from pirate radio stations Radio Caroline and Radio London. He presented the breakfast show on Radio 1 until 1973, regularly hosted *Top of the Pops* and had his own television show, *Time for Blackburn*, in 1968.

Billy Butlin (29 September 1899 – 12 June 1980)

Billy Butlin was an entrepreneur who founded the Butlin's holiday camps throughout the British Isles. The first camp was opened in 1936. The camps reopened after the war and by the 1950s were hugely successful – they were the destination for many British holidaymakers. One of Butlin's slogans was 'a week's holiday for a week's pay'. Billy Butlin retired in 1969, handing the business over to his son, Bobby.

Max Bygraves (16 October 1922 – 31 August 2012)

Max Bygraves was an English entertainer, comedian, singer and actor. Bygraves appeared in several radio shows during the 1950s, including *Educating Archie*, and also appeared in films including *Tom Brown's Schooldays* (1951), *Charley Moon* (1956) and *Bobbikins* (1959). He achieved television fame from the 1950s onwards appearing in shows such as *Whack-O*, *The Royal Variety Performance* and *It's Sad About Eddie*. He also had his own television shows, which included *Max* (1969–74). His hit singles included 'You Need Hands', 'Tulips from Amsterdam' and 'Fings Ain't Wot They Used T'be'.

Michael Caine (born 14 March 1933)

Michael Caine made his film breakthrough in the 1960s, with blockbusters such as *Zulu* (1964), *Alfie* (1966) and *The Italian Job* ('You're only supposed to blow the bloody doors off!', 1969). *Zulu*, which also starred Stanley Baker, was Caine's first major role and depicted the Battle of Rorke's Drift. It cast Caine as Lieutenant Gonville Bromhead.

Fidel Castro (born 13 August 1926)

Fidel Castro was prime minister of Cuba between 1959 and 1976 and president from 1976 until 2008. Alarmed by his allegiances with Russia, US presidents Dwight D. Eisenhower and John F. Kennedy tried unsuccessfully to oust him from power, leading to the Cuban Missile Crisis in 1962.

Michael Collins (born 1930)

Michael Collins was the third member of the Apollo 11 team although he was the only crew member not to walk on the Moon. His first spaceflight had taken place on Gemini 10 in

1966, a mission commanded by John Young. In 1970, Collins retired from NASA.

Sean Connery (born 25 August 1930)

Sean Connery, 'Bond, James Bond', is best remembered for this iconic role during the 1960s. Undoubtedly the best Bond ever, he captured not only the role but the feel of the 1960s. He starred in seven films as Bond between 1962 and 1983. Other films Connery made in the decade included *The Longest Day* (1962), *The Hill* (1965) and *Shalako* (1968).

Charlie Drake (19 June 1925 – 23 December 2006)

Charlie Drake was a popular comedian both on the radio and television from the 1950s until the 1970s. His catchphrase 'Hello my darlings!' was repeated in playgrounds throughout the land. His first television appearance was in *The Centre Show* in 1953. Many more television series followed with, perhaps, *The Worker* being his best known. Drake turned to straight acting in the 1980s and retired in 1995 after suffering a stroke.

Dick Emery (19 February 1915 – 2 January 1983)

Dick Emery was a well-known radio star during the 1950s, appearing in shows like *Workers' Playtime*. His television debut came in *The Centre Show* in 1950 and he then appeared regularly on television, signing a contract with the BBC to star in *The Dick Emery Show* between 1963 and 1981.

Hughie Green (2 February 1920 – 3 May 1997)

Hughie Green is fondly remembered for being the host of many game shows and the talent show *Opportunity Knocks*. He was born in London and had his own BBC radio show by the age of fourteen. He devised the show *Opportunity Knocks* in 1949 and hosted it on radio for one series before being told that it was too American for a British audience. He became a household name with the 1955 television show *Double Your Money* for ITV. The following year, *Opportunity Knocks* first appeared on television. His catchphrase on the show was 'and

I mean that most sincerely, folks'. Green died of lung cancer in 1997.

Tony Hancock (12 May 1924 – 24 June 1968)
Tony Hancock was a comedian and actor best known for his shows on radio and television, including *Hancock's Half Hour* and *The Tony Hancock Show*. He is best remembered for 'The Blood Donor' and 'The Radio Ham' which were episodes from his BBC show, *Hancock* which broadcast in 1961. Although he was one of the best comedians of the time, he was very self critical. He detached himself from many things that made his act so clever, including his writers Galton and Simpson and co-stars Sid James and Kenneth Williams. Hancock took an overdose of amylo-barbitone tablets in Sydney, Australia, and died on 24 June 1968.

Kenneth Horne (27 February 1907 – 14 February 1969)
A comedian who first appeared on the radio in *Much Binding in the Marsh*, which was written by his friend, Richard Murdoch. He is best remembered for his two further radio shows, *Beyond Our Ken* (1958–64) and *Round the Horne* (1965–68). His television appearances included *What's My Line?*, *Ken's Column* and *Call My Bluff* (as a team captain). He also appeared in various specials with Richard Murdoch.

Geoff Hurst (born 8 December 1941)
Geoff Hurst famously scored a hat-trick in the final of the World Cup in 1966, leading England to beat West Germany 4-2, therefore winning the World Cup. He played much of his career with West Ham United before moving to Stoke in 1972.

David Jacobs (19 May 1926 – 2 September 2013)
An actor and broadcaster who appeared in the popular 1950s BBC radio show *Journey into Space*. He was also a disc jockey at Radio Luxembourg and went on to present *Juke Box Jury* (1959–67) on BBC television; he hosted the BBC's programme *Pick of the Pops* on the radio from 1955 until

1962. He's presented many television programmes over the years, including *Song for Europe* (1957–66) and *What's My Line*, which was revived in 1973.

Sid James (8 May 1913 – 26 April 1976)

An actor much loved for his appearance in the Carry On films. He made his name as Tony Hancock's sidekick in *Hancock's Half Hour*. His first major film role was alongside Alfie Bass in *The Lavender Hill Mob* (1951). The movie also starred Alec Guinness and Stanley Holloway. He also appeared in Charlie Chaplin's *A King in New York* (1957) as well as appearing in several other films. His success in the Carry On films led to his own television series, *Bless This House*, which was extremely popular in the 1970s.

C. S. Lewis (29 November 1898 – 22 November 1963)

Clive Staples Lewis was a novelist, poet and academic, and is best known for *The Chronicles of Narnia*, of which the first, *The Lion, the Witch and the Wardrobe*, is his best-known work. His books were greatly enjoyed by children in the 1960s and have been read by millions of people all over the world.

Spike Milligan (16 April 1918 – 27 February 2002)

A founder member of *The Goons*, Milligan was a comedian, writer and musician. He began his radio career writing material for comedian Derek Roy, before famously joining forces with Peter Sellers, Harry Secombe and Michael Bentine, performing as *The Goons*. The first show was broadcast on 28 May 1951 and became an immediate success. Milligan went on to write and appear in many other radio and television shows.

Roger Moore (born 14 October 1927)

Remembered mainly for his roles in *The Saint* and James Bond, Moore began his television career in *Ivanhoe* (1958) and later appeared in *Maverick* (1957–62). He found worldwide fame after he was cast as Simon Templar in *The Saint* (1962–70).

During the 1970s, he appeared with Tony Curtis in *The Persuaders* before taking the lead as James Bond in *Live and Let Die* (1973). He continued to play James Bond until 1985.

Jon Pertwee (7 July 1919 – 20 May 1996)
Jon Pertwee started his radio career appearing as Chief Petty Officer Pertwee in *The Navy Lark*, a show which lasted eighteen years, starting in 1959. He also appeared in many films, including four Carry On movies: *Carry On Cleo* (1964), *Carry On Screaming* (1966), *Carry On Cowboy* (1965) and *Carry On Columbus* (1992).

Elvis Presley (8 January 1935 – 16 August 1977)
Elvis Presley, 'the King of Rock and Roll', was born in Tupelo, Mississippi, in 1935. His many hits, including 'Heartbreak Hotel', 'Hound Dog' and 'Blue Suede Shoes', won him fans all over the world. He caused much controversy with his hip swivelling in the 1950s, and was filmed from the waist up only on the *Ed Sullivan Show*. Presley went on to have many more hit singles in the 1960s and 1970s and appeared in many films. He died at just forty-two years old in 1977.

Harry Secombe (8 September 1921 – 11 April 2001)
A Welsh actor and comedian who was a member of *The Goons* and was famous for his character Neddie Seagoon, central to the show between 1951 and 1960. He appeared in musicals such as *Oliver!* as well as other films. He had several hit singles, including 'If I Ruled the World'. His own television show, *The Harry Secombe Show*, debuted on Christmas Day in 1968. He also hosted religious shows, including *Songs of Praise* and *Highway*.

Peter Sellers (8 September 1925 – 24 July 1980)
During the 1950s, Sellers joined Spike Milligan, Harry Secombe and Michael Bentine as part of the BBC's radio show *The Goons*. He had previously made his radio debut after the war on a programme called *ShowTime*. He also appeared in films, including *Dr Strangelove* (1964), *What's New,*

Pussycat? (1965), *Casino Royale* (1967) and the Inspector
Clouseau Pink Panther films, which were made between 1963
and 1978. He died on 24 July 1980, aged fifty-four, after
suffering a heart attack.

Andy Warhol (6 August 1928 – 22 February 1987)
Andy Warhol was a leading figure in the pop art movement
that flourished in the 1960s. Among his best-known works
are those of Campbell's soup cans and iconic pop art works of
Marilyn Monroe, Muhammad Ali and Elizabeth Taylor. He
famously predicted that 'in the future everyone will be world-
famous for fifteen minutes'.

Jack Warner (24 October 1895 – 24 May 1981)
Jack Warner was a film and television actor who found fame
and became a household name while appearing in *Dixon of
Dock Green* (famous for George Dixon's catchphrase 'Evening
all'). The show ran from 1955 until 1976 and was extremely
popular with television audiences. He also appeared in many
movies over the years. Warner died in 1981, aged eighty-five.

Adam West (born 19 September 1928)
Adam West gained fame as Batman in the 1966–68 television
series of the same name. Burt Ward starred alongside him as
Robin. The show was hugely successful and featured many
colourful villains, including The Riddler (played by Frank
Gorshin and John Astin), The Penguin (played by Burgess
Meredith), The Joker (played by Cesar Romero) and Catwoman
(played by Julie Newmar, Eartha Kitt and Lee Meriwether).

The Who
The Who included Roger Daltrey (born in March 1944),
Pete Townsend (born May 1945), John Entwistle (9 October
1944–27 June 2002) and Keith Moon (23 August 1946–7
September 1978). Along with The Beatles and The Rolling
Stones, they are regarded as one of the most important rock
bands of their time. Hits included 'I Can't Explain', 'My
Generation' and 'I Can See for Miles'.

Kenneth Williams (22 February 1926 – 15 April 1988)
Kenneth Williams was a comedian, actor and writer who appeared in many radio and television shows featuring Tony Hancock and Kenneth Horne. Providing funny voices for the show, Williams found fame in *Hancock's Half Hour*. He later appeared on *Beyond Our Ken* and *Round the Horne*. He is best remembered for the many Carry On films he appeared in during the 1960s and 1970s. He regularly appeared on television and wrote several best-selling books.

Acknowledgements

Thanks to Darrell Burge for permission to use the Hornby, Airfix, Humbrol, Corgi and Scalextric adverts, Black Cat Firework Limited for use of the Standard Fireworks advert and Sacha da Cunha Soars for use of the Letraset Action Transfers advert.

Thanks also to Flickr user 'Combom'. I have tried to track down all copyright holders of photos and illustrations used and apologise to anyone who hasn't been mentioned.